Mind-Spirit Detox

Reboot, reset and recharge with
40 beautiful practices to deepen
your oneness with Spirit

Mind-Spirit Detox

Reboot, reset and recharge with
40 beautiful practices to deepen
your oneness with Spirit

Richard Charles Anderson

BOOKS

Winchester, UK
Washington, USA

First published by O-Books, 2019
O-Books is an imprint of John Hunt Publishing Ltd., 3 East St., Alresford,
Hampshire SO24 9EE, UK
office1@jhpbooks.net
www.johnhuntpublishing.com

For distributor details and how to order please visit the 'Ordering' section on our website.

Text copyright: Richard Charles Anderson 2018

ISBN: 978 1 78904 044 9
978 1 78904 045 6 (ebook)
Library of Congress Control Number: 2018932824

A CIP catalogue record for this book is available from the British Library.

Photos and Cover Design Copyright © 2018 Richard C Anderson

Design: Cecilia Perriard

Printed and bound by CPI Group (UK) Ltd, Croydon, CR0 4YY, UK

We operate a distinctive and ethical publishing philosophy in
all areas of our business, from our global network of authors to
production and worldwide distribution.

Contents

Awakening Coaching UK

To my father for your deep wisdom
and leading me in my spiritual awakening;
to my mother for your steadfastness and love;
to Isabel for your beauty and vision;
to Thalia for your strength and confidence;
to Sophie for your purity and spirit;
and to Emily for your indomitable
bounciness and absolute certainty.

Foreword

Richard Anderson is a fresh and distinct voice in the field of practical spirituality. Grounded in the Christian tradition with a sensitive appreciation of scripture, he combines this approach with a knowledge and experiential understanding of the unitive path with its emphasis on psychological subtlety, practical mysticism and universality.

In each of the 40 chapters that make up the book, Richard skillfully presents ways in which we can explore the key theme and mine its meaning on many levels. Using an honest, natural and conversational style of writing, yet one that is impeccable in its precision, he invites us to reason and contemplate the theme, and then experience it directly through beautiful guided meditations and affirmations.

Richard is gifted in his ability to share with clarity and compassion. I am pleased to write a foreword for this book and celebrate his achievement in bringing so much spiritual wisdom to all those seeking a spirituality that embraces and unifies; one that reminds us that love prevails and that our prime and joyous task is to be co-creators with the Divine Spirit.

Rev. Paul John Roach MA
Minister, radio show host, writer, spiritual counsellor and environmental activist
Fort Worth, Texas

Why Detox?

My intention in writing this book is for you to realise the full power, beauty, peace and purpose that is your 'higher good'. I absolutely know that this 'good' is already there...it is inside you right now. However, it may be concealed under all of the thoughts and memories and habitual mind-programs that have accumulated in your life over the years. Your mind and your spirit occasionally need a bit of a detox!

You might have been on the spiritual path for some time, trying to overcome perceived issues of lack, or distance from God. You may even have read countless books that purport to solve your issues, or have attended conferences and seminars. The problem with many of these, however, is that they often outline a very compelling vision, a picture of how life could be, certainly how life seems to be for the writer or speaker. But what they often leave out is exactly how to get to B from A, a road map from here to there.

My will is that this book will change your life, that you will see an incredible expansion of spirit, of love, and of compassion in your daily walk; you will come to know your deepest purpose on this earth, and this purpose will be firmly rooted in the Divine breath of Spirit. Contained within the 40 practices in this book are practical ideas and exercises which will clear out the old, used-up energy, the accumulated debris of false beliefs and unhelpful thoughts that separate you from your true nature, and from universal truth. The good news is that access to this state is actually very simple, but the paradox is that even though it is hidden in full sight, most people, most of the time, either can't find it, don't know it's there, or simply don't care.

Given that you've bought this book, presumably none of the latter applies to you. However, the question remains: why doesn't all of this come more naturally to us? Why isn't it easier for us to connect with our truest self, with Spirit and with our ultimate purpose in life?

Nowadays we often feel such disconnection in these vital relationships. There are so many things that build up in our lives like toxins in the body. This could be anger, frustration, stress, addiction or simply the burn-out of everyday life. Either way, if this happens in the body, we know what to do – see the doctor, hit the health spa, or go on a diet. But when the build-up is deeper within, what do we do? How do we start?

The monotony of daily routine can trap us in a cyclical habit of event-reaction. It's as if our subconscious is stuck in a pre-programmed response. How then do we break this habit? How can we return to happiness? How can we connect with Spirit, with God? Is it even possible to feel like you're the best version of yourself?

Just think about it – there are so many things that we do on a daily basis, such as brush our teeth, shower, eat, maybe exercise. We do this to stay healthy. We have to do so; if we don't then we neglect ourselves, and we will become moribund and sick. So why do we think for a moment that we can develop a healthy relationship with our inner self and with God if we neglect the pursuit of spiritual maintenance tasks on a daily basis?

This is where spiritual practice comes in. Practice brings presence and consciousness; it brings awareness, insight and growth. It detoxes the mind-spirit system. If you don't practise, then you only have automatic conditioning to fall back on.

The practices in this book are based upon ancient spiritual teaching as well as some new and emerging discoveries. They will reward you with beautiful insight into the reality both of who you are, and the true nature of God, or 'What Is'. These practices will further your understanding in your spiritual walk and they will mend your relationship with Spirit and begin to dispel any lingering doubt as belief morphs into knowledge, and as head-located thought shifts to heart-felt understanding.

You will move from relying on the crutch of dead routine and unconscious faith as you develop a new outlook, a freshness, a beautiful flourishing in your personal relationship with Spirit.

When we turn to practice, we begin to feel the divine reality of Spirit within us. Spiritual practices open portals to the Divine. The introduction of practice into our daily life brings us into touch systematically with the inner core of who we really are and what we're doing here at this time on this planet. Practice opens us up to the flow of Spirit in our thoughts, words and actions. It brings us into the 'now', and away from living in thoughts of the future, or regrets of the past.

But let's not be too hard on ourselves. We are human after all, and humanity has its weaknesses. As such, there is a very compelling reason in our frailty as people as to why we let passivity take us over. Before embarking on this book, it's vitally important that this is understood.

The reason for avoidance of practice is that we have a multitude of 'persons' inside ourselves. There is a constant battle between the person who has great intentions, who wants to develop, to grow and to improve, and the person who just can't be bothered, who'd rather check email or watch TV; so often, therefore, resistance blocks intention. That's why I've written these practices to be fun, engaging, never onerous, and to let you see rapid results. These 40 practices are designed to align with the new renaissance of spirit. They will enable you to expand your intuition and to allow the full movement of God to become a visceral reality in your own life, right here, right now.

* * *

A brief note on how to undertake these practices. I would urge you not to rush. This book is one to be savoured at a natural pace. Let the truths sink into your heart and mind. This is a practical book; it isn't just about understanding theory and concepts. I would urge you to absorb the deepest meaning of each chapter through the window of the heart, before it even reaches the head. As such, don't just do the practices once and discard them – you can return to them time and time again.

Gentle pace and contemplation is the key. Contemplation is one of the three key ways of being that bring light to the path of truth. The other two are meditation and concentration. Let me explain.

Starting with meditation, this is a right-brained, holistic activity. It is about going within, and witnessing 'what is'. It is an effortless activity in which you just accept that everything that arises is perfect. Many of the practices in this book involve meditation. After meditative practice, as we go about our daily lives, the lens of contemplation will magnify the effects of meditation back into the manifest realm.

On the other end of the spectrum, we have concentration. This is the left-brained activity that looks at logic and sequence. Much effort is needed. Indeed, when thinking becomes concentrated, we actually use 20% of our overall calorie expenditure by brain activity alone! That explains why we get so tired when we concentrate for extensive periods of time. Concentration is involved in understanding dogma and doctrine and working through the logic of scriptural theology. It is used in understanding and remembering Bible verses and narrative. While you may have cause to concentrate within some of these practices, remember to keep this activity in its rightful place. This book is about coming closer to the Divine within each one of us. There are times when concentration helps us in this understanding, but use it as a temporary vehicle; do not let it absorb the space which should be devoted to feeling with the heart. I would encourage you to shift your awareness and your processing capacity from your head to your heart. In this way, practice creates a new reality within the soul – understanding and insight will genuinely shift who you are at a fundamental heart level.

How frequently do we attempt to understand spiritual wisdom with our human intellect...it will not work. Truth is not a reasoning process; therefore, it must be spiritually discerned. Truth does not as a rule appeal to our reason, and when it appears to do so, we must search deeply to see if it really is truth.

– Joel S Goldsmith, *The Infinite Way*

Contemplation, on the other hand, is something of a middle way; it's a bit of a lost art. It uses components of both meditation and concentration, and it harnesses the power of both. It is less structured and formal, and it can be incorporated into everyday life. It is designed for normal people living normal lives. Just let the truth of the practices drip into your soul. Realisation of truth and the connection you make with your higher self and Spirit will seep into you and revelation will explode into your soul when you least expect it. The deepest Truths, when incorporated through practice into your daily routine, will infuse your everyday, lived existence with Divine Spirit.

As you work with these practices, you will discover how life can be when you live it in true knowledge and realisation of who you are, your place in time and space, in relationship to God, in relationship with other people, and above all, in relation to your true, deepest essence. When you arrive in this place, you will discover that there is nothing there, i.e. all thought disappears, all concept of the 'self' disappears. All you are left with is the 'see-er', the 'I-am-ness' of self, of pure subjectivity. And in that nothingness, you will find the everything, the heart of *you* and the heart of Spirit. The 'singularity' is what I call the conscious meeting place of you and The Universe, hence the 'everything'. While here on earth as a spirit in human form, we only really ever get fleeting glimpses of this singularity, but in those brief passages of time, we experience the most expansive, beautiful moments that can carry us through the rest of life.

Lastly, note that some of the practices take the form of meditation best carried out with your eyes closed. You can imagine that it is rather difficult to do this and read the meditation at the same time! As such, why not have a look at www.awakeningcoaching.co.uk where you will find many of the meditations in audible form? Also, please check out my YouTube channel, under my name, Richard C Anderson, or click on: https://www.youtube.com/channel/UCuqvuz3C7FzbLXTx7VBMqog/videos?view_as=subscriber

Here you will find more Mind-Spirit Detox videos to accompany this book, as well as a plethora of book reviews in the field of spirituality, science and human development.

If you want to go even further, please subscribe to my blog and my Facebook site, Awakening Coaching UK.

So, enjoy the practices, play with them, relish them. Read at your own pace, contemplate with an open and loving heart; let your heart sing and let Spirit in!

Enjoy your journey!

1

Let it Go

Let all bitterness and wrath and anger and clamour and slander be put away from you, along with all malice. Be kind to one another, tender-hearted, forgiving one another, as God in Christ forgave you.
– Ephesians 4:31–32

You will find that it is necessary to let things go; simply for the reason that they are heavy. So let them go, let go of them. I tie no weights to my ankles.
– C. JoyBell C.

Practice:
I would encourage you to read and re-read the above quotes. After 'be kind to one another', add, 'be kind to yourself'. Forgive yourself and make yourself clean of self-judgement.

Take a notebook or a diary.
Go into a quiet place.
Find space for yourself and go within.
Search for any self-limiting beliefs.
These may include things such as:
- I'm not good enough
- There's never enough time
- I'm not good-looking enough
- Nobody really loves me
- I'll never amount to anything
- People are always judging me
Keep at it; this will take time.
If you really search deeply within, you can find scores of

these beliefs.

If in doubt as to whether it's a belief or not, ask yourself, 'If I asked 1,000 people if this was definitively true, would all 1,000 say "yes"?'

If that's *not* the case, i.e. not everybody agrees that it is definitively the truth, then it's just a Point of View.

Now contemplate this: A Point of View isn't true or untrue; it's just a point of view. It's an opinion or a belief.

So, we can't say whether that belief is true or untrue, but we can ask whether it serves our higher purpose or not.

Now, look at each Point of View and consider whether it serves your higher purpose. Does it make your soul sing? Does it make your heart dance? If not, then it's probably not serving your higher purpose.

Write Y or N next to each one, according to whether you can answer Yes or No to this question, i.e. is the Point of View serving your higher purpose, your higher good?

For those with a 'N', ask yourself the question, 'What would life look like if I didn't hold on to this Point of View?' Really feel into this. See what your life would look like, feel what your life would be like; live it in your mind.

If you like what you see, now ask yourself the question, 'Could I let it go?' Just *could* you?

Now think of any little child that you know. Would you give them this Point of View as a gift?

Would you choose this Point of View for yourself from a menu, if you had a menu full of Points of View rather than food?!

Is there any by-law where you live that says that you have to hold on to this Point of View?

If you can answer 'No' to all of these questions, then ask yourself again, 'Can I let it go?' It is neither true nor untrue; you've established that it isn't serving your higher purpose. You have permission to let it go.

So just let it go!

Close your eyes. Go within. See the Point of View. With the out-breath, just let it go from your body; release it into the air like a puff of wind. Wave it goodbye.

You might want to conduct a burning bowl ceremony of the Points of View. Write each one on a piece of paper. Cut them up into individual Points of View. Put them in a fireproof bowl or into the fireplace. Set them aflame!

Another beautiful technique is called the 'Energy Conversion Box'.

At its most basic form, your body is made up of atoms; atoms are nearly entirely empty of matter, but they are buzzing with energy. You know what energy is released when the atom is split? That's how much energy there is in your body, and we have 7,000,000,000,000,000,000,000,000,000 atoms in our body, so we have unimaginable amounts of energy inside us!

These Points of View are manifestations of the negative energy that is harboured within you. The Energy Conversion Box converts this energy by releasing the negative.

Go into a meditative state. Build yourself your own Energy Conversion Box in your mind.

Make this box your own, but you have to imagine a large, solid box, like an old trunk, with a very heavy lid. Get all the Points of View that do not serve you and just get in the way, and put them into the Energy Conversion Box. Close the heavy lid and lock it. Now imagine pushing the box away with the force of an elephant; the box fizzes away into eternity and disappears down into nothingness. It is gone forever, together with all of its contents.

Can you feel the weight lifting from you now? None of these Points of View are any longer attached to you. You are free. Free to be the person that you were always meant to be; free to give your gift; free to let Spirit fully into every corner of your heart, mind and body.

Give yourself a reward now – you've earned it; this is the beginning of the rest of your life. Let your heart sing and dance; let your love and your spirit shine.

* * *

We are riddled with Points of View – these are self-limiting beliefs; baggage; hurts; things that have been done and said to us that we have chosen consciously or subconsciously to hold on to. We harbour these beliefs in our heart, in our mind and in our soul.

This is an extensive practice and it might take many days, if not many weeks, to come near to completion. I have suggested different ways of letting these Points of View go. You might like to think of your own; some people even imagine flushing each one down the lavatory!

Freeing yourself of these unhealthy beliefs can be one of the most important and liberating things that we ever do. Many people live their entire lives as slaves to these beliefs. For example, some people think that there's never enough money. They might devote all of their life to trying to make more wealth, and feeling constantly weighed down by this thought. Other people might think that they're too ugly; they might spend a fortune on plastic surgery, or expend lots of negative energy worrying about what others might think of them. Some people think that all of their energy has to be used in service of others, in constantly giving, and never taking any time to heal themselves.

That's why this practice often takes some time. You are overcoming a lifetime of stored baggage. This isn't solved in a day. Keep your notebook close by, or start a page in 'Notes' on your smartphone. Just be really aware of your thoughts, and whenever something pops into your head, write it down.

Once you begin to let these self-limiting beliefs go, it's amazing how much freer you are to let Spirit in; to explore who you really are; to grow in spirit and as a person, and to give your gift to the world.

Many traditionally religious people deny the need to do exercises such as this; they say that all they need to do is let God in and all will be swept clean. But if they are still riddled with these self-limiting beliefs, then they never offer a clean slate upon which God can truly work. As a result, they might say the same prayer over and over for years, but it never truly works, because this negative energy is getting in the way.

Much of this book is about two aspects: truly knowing ourselves, and truly knowing God, or 'What Is', or the Absolute Truth. The problem we often have is that sacred texts tell us only the end point, but not always so much about the detail of how to get there. These practices are straightforward ways in which we can free ourselves from the tyranny of self-limiting belief; truly to get to know who we are and what our place is in the world; to know our own purpose and let Sprit in.

This practice is one of the more extensive and important ways in which we can give ourselves a really good spring-clean. Enjoy the results!

Contemplate:
- How was it to realise that you have the option of letting these Points of View go?
- How did it feel to release them?
- Were you surprised at how many Points of View you discovered?

2

Consciously Express Love

Love is patient and kind...Love bears all things, believes all things, hopes all things, endures all things.
– 1 Corinthians 13:4–7

Your task is not to seek for love, but merely to seek and find all the barriers within yourself that you have built against it.
– Rumi

Practice:
If you are in a relationship, practise consciously giving love three to four times a day.

This isn't dependent on how you feel.

Just *give!*

Even if you're not in the mood, take ten minutes out and sit with your partner.

Listen to them without distraction.

Be with them.

Or look into their eyes and tell them that you love them deeply.

Or tell them that they're looking really beautiful.

Give them a kiss.

* * *

It is important to understand love as a *feeling* versus love as a *practice* (as a discipline). If your wife or husband isn't looking so hot and you don't get a feeling, a frisson of love or fancying them in the moment, it doesn't matter. Tell them that they are beautiful anyway. In this way, you're not simply responding to a feeling of love, or a sight of beauty; you are actually *creating* the love and the beauty.

Your partner can become the arena in which you practise love. When you get better at it, then this can begin to flow over to other people.

If you just do normal things with your partner, then that's just being normal. However, if you do things to develop your relationship, then that's a practice. A practice is therefore a conscious and systematic engagement with yourself, with God or with another person.

Being loving because you're having an emotion is different from practising love because you want to create that, because you want to *create* the love. It's the difference between *creative/ proactive/conscious* love and *unconscious/reactive* love. Most people have at one time fallen in love, and we feel naturally like we're entitled to natural love all of the time, but life just doesn't work that way. So many marriages fail when both partners believe that they are entitled to love, and when they believe that the love that they show the other person needs no conscious effort, no creativity.

In some ways, when love is practised consciously, it produces and reflects a deeper love, as it comes from a deep well of creativity and intention. You're giving love into the world, where otherwise there wouldn't be love. You're saying, 'Hey, I want to feel love; I want to create, grow and develop this relationship', rather than saying, 'I feel love and I am reacting to it.'

Thus we can see that love is not only a reactive feeling, but it can also be a creative action.

If you are spending some time listening to your partner, this practice shifts your intention from listening because you feel like listening, towards listening as a loving gift to your partner.

Similarly, if you're complimenting your partner on his or her inner and/or outer beauty, you are showing appreciation not because you see and react to the beauty, but because you're committed to creating beauty. You're appreciating something you want to bring forth, rather than something that's already there.

You can do this with other family members or friends, colleagues, neighbours and acquaintances as well. For example, if a teenager is lying to you, if you say, 'You're a liar', then you're reinforcing the identity of what you don't want. You can create beauty by giving appreciation for the beauty before it's there. You create the beauty. You are consciously shifting energy and creating love.

I believe that we not only are *able* to do this, but moreover, we have a *duty* to consciously co-create love; co-creating with Spirit. There can be no higher calling for us.

So, show love, give space, give affirmations to the people close to you. Do it as an act of generosity and honour to the Divine and to that person.

Contemplate:
- Can you see how there isn't a fixed stock of love? Can you see how you are able to increase love and happiness and joy and connection in yourself and in those around you?
- If God is pure love, can you recognise how this connects you with the living Spirit of love in the Universe?

3

Love and Fear

There is no fear in love. But perfect love drives out fear, because fear has to do with punishment. The one who fears is not made perfect in love.
– 1 John 4:18, NIV

Life begins where fear ends.
– Osho

Practice:
Over the course of a few days, keep a notebook close by (or notes in your smartphone).
Be aware of everything that you do and say.
Feel into the motivation behind everything.
What drives you to say or do it?
Is it love?
Or is it fear?
When you notice a strong sense of love or fear, write it down.
Look for patterns.
What is behind your words and deeds?
What effect did it have on those around you?
What effect did it have on you?

* * *

There are two basic motivating forces: fear and love. When we are afraid, we pull back from life. When we are in love, we open to all that life has to offer with passion, excitement, and acceptance. We need to learn to love ourselves first, in all our glory and our imperfections. If we cannot love ourselves, we cannot fully open to our ability to love others or our potential to create. Evolution and all hopes for a better world rest in the fearlessness and open-hearted vision of people who embrace life.

– John Lennon

Love is your higher self. It is the highest vibration of all. It is the place of pure intention and infinite possibility. When your higher self drives your life, you are 'on purpose' and empowered. Life and love surges through you; you thrive and all people you touch begin to thrive as well. Love and fear are both contagious.

Fear is love's opposite and comes from the lowest of vibrations. So many of us live from the place of fear. This practice is a way in which we can become aware of what it is that drives us. It brings us into conscious realisation of what we may already half-know in our subconscious.

Feel into yourself and what lies behind your actions and your words; what lies behind your behaviour. Do you feel that you are a victim? Do you feel that people are looking at you and judging you? Do you feel that bad things might happen to you? Are you afraid of people and their intentions? Then you may be living from a place of fear. Your lower self, your lower vibrations, may be driving your life.

Alternatively, if you feel compassion and love towards other people; if you have a sense of expansiveness and possibility; if you feel aligned between your hopes and your daily actions; if you feel a connection between the little actions you carry out every day and your higher purpose and your gifts, then you're living a life driven by higher vibration, by love.

The latter are more obvious manifestations of love and of fear. They are examples at either end of the polarity. Now look deeper. Seek the half-hidden expressions somewhere between both ends of the polarity. Love and fear sometimes present themselves in subtle ways. Feel into events and reactions in your daily life and reflect on which side of the polarity they are closest to.

If you feel goodwill towards others; if you feel yourself smiling; if laughter comes easily; if you live in communion with others; if you feel energy flowing through you, then this all lives in the 'love' end of the polarity.

If, however, you feel rushes of adrenaline; if you are hesitant to allow instinct to flow naturally; if you get feelings of worthlessness and lack; if you feel shy to bring forth feelings; if you try to dampen down inspiration, if you feel the tyranny of peer-pressure, then maybe these are driven by lower vibrations and fear.

Practice:

Once you have kept a diary for about a week, look at the balance.

Is your higher vibrational self, i.e. love, driving your life?

Or is your lower vibrational self squeezing this out, like weeds taking over healthy plants?

If the love isn't flourishing, use the 'Affirm the Truth' and 'Deny Falsehoods' practices to pronounce the truth:

Your life is beautiful,

You are powerful beyond measure,

This world needs your gifts; your brilliance; your genius.

Affirm that you will live according to your higher good.

Deny fear any stranglehold over your life.

Deny any self-limiting belief.

Instruct fear to leave.

Tell it that it has no place in your life.

Reach for the sky.

Be the person that Spirit always intended you to be.

* * *

Once you have done this, it is a practice that you may have to repeat several times. In fact, research suggests that it can take around two months of daily practice to cement a new habit or a new way of looking at things psychologically. So it might take some time, but gradually, you should find that a combination of the in-working of Spirit and rewiring of the brain begins to bring forth love and positivity into your life as key drivers. This gives you a beautiful new weed-free pasture upon which any new plants in your life can grow in abundance!

Contemplate:

- If you get stuck in a situation, just ask yourself, 'What would love do?'
- You could also ask, 'What is my higher self asking me to do?' In this vein, if you find yourself stuck in unhelpful patterns of thought, use these quick-fire, powerful affirmations to pull yourself back into alignment with your higher good:

     'Awareness now'
     'Higher self now'

- Do you feel your lower self trying to reduce or contract your highest purpose? If so, then reject it. Tell it to go away; tell it that you have committed your life to the higher purpose.
- If you still get stuck, ask yourself the question, 'What would my life look like if it was driven by love?' Just having a vision of this is 'psychoactive' and might be enough to kick-start the conscious shift in your life towards the higher vibration.
- How does it feel for you when you make the shift and let love be the higher power in your life?
- How does it feel to dissipate the power of fear? To be in control of fear?

- Once you have got into the habit of letting the higher power of love be the dominant driver in your life, feel into it – do you feel your light shining brighter? What other ways does this manifest for you? For example, heavy versus light; expansion versus contraction; infinite possibility versus constant limitation.

4

Grace and the Three 'Thank Yous'

Giving thanks always and for everything...
– Ephesians 5:20

The report of this came to the ears of the church in Jerusalem, and they sent Barnabas to Antioch. When he came and saw the grace of God, he was glad, and he exhorted them all to remain faithful to the Lord with steadfast purpose, for he was a good man, full of the Holy Spirit and of faith. And a great many people were added to the Lord.
– Acts 11:22–24

Happiness is the spiritual experience of living every minute with love, grace and gratitude.
– Denis Waitley

Practice:
Every night when you go to bed, as you close your eyes, simply say 'thank you' for three things.

These could be coincidences and synchronicities that have happened to you that day (not forgetting that there's no such thing as a 'coincidence' that hasn't been pre-planned by your team of Angels!).

It could be for relationships that have formed.

It could be for the chance you had to influence others in the Spirit of God.

It could be for simple pleasures that you experienced.

It could be for anything and everything.

Let your heart guide you.

* * *

It is often said that if we say only one prayer every day, then we should let it be a prayer of 'thanks'. Not only is it the most powerful prayer we can say, but moreover, it helps root our consciousness in grace.

So, what is grace? Put simply, it means to get something that you do not deserve. It is unmerited favour. Remember, you are an eternal conscious spirit. No money in the entire Universe would be enough to buy what that is worth. From the tiniest thing, such as feeling the beauty in a smile, through to standing before the majesty of a mountain, we experience the grace of pure life every second of the day. We may not always be conscious of it; indeed, most of the time we're probably not. It often takes something really big to get us to recognise grace in our lives.

So, for those few moments when you're doing nothing else but resting, just be aware of grace and give thanks for the beauty of existence. The best time to do this is every night as you close your eyes. Practices that you can do in empty down-time are fantastic – there are so many in this book that you can do when you're not really doing anything else; you can use natural space within the day to do this inner work.

So thank God for the constant little miracles that weave in and out of your life every day. Focus on the really small ones as well as the more obvious ones. We are here on earth in human form for such a short amount of time; think about the things that make life in embodied form so wonderful – the taste of popcorn; shafts of sunlight dappling through the leaves of a tree; the sound of laughter; the smell of toast; the feel of a hug.

So just say, 'Thanks'. God loves it. It helps you notice the grace that is so abundant in your life; it's also a brilliant antidote to complaining about the negative. A 'thank you' is infinitely more powerful than a whinge!

Contemplate:
- If you initially think it might be difficult to come up with

three things, why not start a list of things that you are grateful for, things that you haven't earned, that have been given to you by grace. How many things have you got in your list? People are often staggered at just how long a list they have.

- Once you've got going, try keeping a list of the three things that you say 'thank you' for every day. It's a beautiful reference point to look back on at a later stage, or if you're ever feeling sad or negative.

5

Unity

And above all these put on love, which binds everything together in perfect harmony.
– Colossians 3:14

Complete my joy by being of the same mind, having the same love, being in full accord and of one mind.
– Philippians 2:2

...maintain the unity of the Spirit in the bond of peace.
– Ephesians 4:3

No one can live without relationship. You may withdraw into the mountains, become a monk, a sannyasi, wander off into the desert by yourself, but you are related. You cannot escape from that absolute fact. You cannot exist in isolation.
– Krishnamurti

Practice:

At the heart of it all
Lies a unifying truth,
The Great Perfection,
The immaculate Christ,
The mind of the Universe,
The untouched consciousness of all that is;
Enfolding all,
The truth in all,
No division, no joins, no separation,
Enfolding science, art, poetry, the biosphere, music, cognition, cosmology, subtle energies, the world of form and the

world of spirit.

Whatever has been, is and is to come,

This essence of Truth unites all; it is the essence of who we are.

Allow your awareness to rest simply as it is, right now in this very moment.

Know that nothing you have experienced, nothing you are experiencing now, and nothing you can ever experience will in any way change that Great Perfection.

Know that your experience is irrelevant to that Perfection. Nothing that you can do can change your deepest awareness; the see-er inside.

Let your subjective experience be irrelevant to you. Let everything that arises in consciousness simply arise and be whatever it is; let it do whatever it does, and make no attempt to change any of it.

See that Divine Spirit exists in everything, unites everything, and yet remains untouched by anything.

Simply allow it to be.

* * *

Our surroundings aren't just a backdrop. Science isn't an uncomfortable truth that we attempt to push out of our awareness when we connect with Spirit. God *is* science; Spirit transcends and unites the world of form and the untouchable world of consciousness and love.

Our ecological surroundings and our relationship with them are not separate from Spirit. When we hold a leaf from a tree in our hand, we connect directly not only with the biosphere, but also with our creator. Our hands and the hands of God touch in that moment. All around us we can experience these relationships between the world of Spirit and the world of form.

We can describe these as 'holons', that is, something that is simultaneously a part and a whole.

Too often we think of ourselves as radically individual and separate beings. This is a falsehood – a lie. Every atom in our body is made of stardust, created after the Big Bang. Every cell in our body interacts with every other body in the Universe. Our emotions interact with the emotions of every other being.

Every time you breathe in, you're breathing in over 4 trillion molecules that were once breathed by Jesus. Scientists have estimated that 227 of these were actually in his very last breath. Your words connect you with countless other people. Every time you have a non-dual experience, when you connect with the vast open spaciousness of awareness, you are in touch with every other being in the Universe.

Your body, every feeling, every thought and spirit itself is swimming in a network of being, the consciousness of the Universe. The Universe is not a dead machine, but a wildly alive, creative, emergent, evolutionary spirit in action.

As well as *growing up* (i.e. knowing with our head who we are, who God is, the relationship of Spirit and science), we also need to *wake up* to who and what we really are. When we wake up, we grow our spiritual intelligence and direct, conscious awareness of God – we connect at the deepest level with the presence of Spirit. When we do this at the most profound metaphysical levels, we connect with the very creation of the Universe itself. When this happens, we experience the binding together of everything, all that exists, the world of form and the world of Spirit, in a grand unifying holon; all division, all duality melts away and we know God as the totality of all that is. This is true freedom, true unity *of* all and *in* all.

Therefore, the spiritual path lying before us prompts us not only to grow up and mature in this unity awareness, but moreover to wake up to successively subtler, more conscious, more loving realms of being, all the way to the ultimate ground of all being – spirit itself, our supreme identity in the Kingdom of God.

Contemplate:

- Did the realisation that there is a fundamental unity of everything create an explosion in your awareness?
- What were the effects of this shift and awakening of consciousness for you?
- How does this change your image of God? Does it expand your knowledge of and relationship with the Divine?

6

Be a Light for the World

No one lights a lamp and then puts it under a basket. Instead, a lamp is placed on a stand, where it gives light to everyone in the house.
– Matthew 5:15, NLT

Practice:

Sit or lie comfortably. Now take several deep breaths and completely relax and let go. Focus on your breathing. With each exhale, just feel yourself moving deeper and deeper into an ideal state to open to Spirit.

Completely relax.

Allow your eyes to close and just imagine that every cell and every system of your body is just letting go and relaxing.

Just continue to focus on your breathing. And with every breath, you are going deeper. With each exhale, just feel yourself letting go, relaxing. Completely.

Now use the unlimited power of your mind, and I want you to imagine that a little light has just appeared within your heart. Just see the light, a little white light within your heart. As you exhale, imagine the light becoming steadily brighter and bigger.

Letting go, relaxing, and as you sink deeper, the light becomes ever brighter, ever brighter.

Now the light becomes so intense that it bursts out of the heart and expands to shine into every corner of your body, illuminating every part of your body.

Feel the light; BE the light. The light is dazzling in its intensity, but you can easily see it; it doesn't hurt your eyes. It's intensely white and luminous. It is warm and protective, pure in spirit, pure in love.

Chapter 6

And as the light grows ever more intense, it begins to illuminate the space around you.

With every out-breath, the light grows. The light of pure Spirit, filling every corner of the room around you.

Rest in the light.

BE the light.

BE the love.

* * *

To understand light and darkness, one must know that the light of God is real; it was there in the beginning, and it lives within each of us. It is the light of Creation and of our own Divine essence. It is who we are at our deepest core. Indeed, each of us are children of the Light and children of God, and the process of Creation that we hold to be true of the past is ongoing, both within the Cosmos and within each individual being.

As well as being 'beings of light', we are also 'beings of love'. Saint Paul tells us to 'walk as children of light'; Saint John tells us that 'the light has come into the world'. Therefore, light and love are intrinsically interwoven in the Bible. As such, this meditative practice is less our imagining what might be in a metaphorical sense, and more about just recognising what we already are – light and love!

Contemplate:

- How does it feel to allow yourself to be pure light?
- Can you take this light into your day-to-day life? Try switching the light on in your heart during the day. Radiate the light to those around you. Notice what happens.

7

I Connect with Earth

It is he who made the earth by his power, who established the world by his wisdom, and by his understanding stretched out the heavens.
– Jeremiah 51:15

The foot feels the foot when it feels the ground.
– Buddha

Practice:
Stand outside, take off your shoes; stand bare-footed on the grass or the sand of the beach.

Feel the earth beneath your feet. The entire planet is under your feet. The entire Universe is above.

If it helps, imagine that you are underneath the planet or on the side, not on top of it. Know that it is only gravity that keeps you anchored to the ground. The planet is connecting with you, pulling you in.

Now, imagine roots growing down from the soles of your feet, extending further and further into the ground as if they were roots of a tree. Down, down, extending the roots further, thick roots, pulling you down and connecting you with the energy and strength of the earth.

Now, breathe deeply. Feel yourself breathing up through the roots. Breathe from the soles of your feet; feel the energy moving up through mother earth into the soles of your feet, up through your legs and filling the very core of your body. Feel the energy expanding up through your head. Feel the power relaxing your body, relaxing your muscles and connecting you with the power of the planet. Feel your thoughts stilling; be at one with this beautiful planet. The earth is connecting with you, talking with you. This beautiful planet that we call home; made for us by the living Spirit of all that is. It is precious; it is the artwork of God. Its power is now filling every fibre of your being.

So, with every in-breath, feel the power of the earth moving through you right up to the top of your head.

With the out-breath, let all stress, all old, used-up energy, release from your body; pushing it higher and higher, up through the top of your head. Let it go, let it float up into the sky, let it climb, let it go, let it go.

Feel your roots continuing to burrow down, ever deeper, down to the very core of the planet. They grow stronger as they go deeper; they stretch wider, ever wider.

Continue to pull energy up through your roots, channelling it up into your heart; fill your heart with the abundant energy of mother earth. With every in-breath, drawing more pure, clear energy; with every out-breath, letting go of all negative thoughts and emotions; any used-up, old energy that no longer serves you.

See the old energy going higher and higher and dissipating on the wind. See it go; it is gone forever.

Just continue to breathe; continue to recycle the old, used-up energy with clean, beautiful, earth energy. Feel your body releasing tension. You become relaxed, energised, connected.

Feel your body fully replenished.

Rest as that.

Feel the connection with mother earth, with your home.

Now, when you are ready, slowly begin to draw your roots back up; feel them rising, rising, and dissolving. Their work is done for now.

Move your body; gently open your eyes.

Know that you have been refreshed by the power of this Divinely created, beautiful planet that we can call home. This organic, fresh and clean energy is now part of you.

Enjoy your walk on the planet today; use the energy wisely.

* * *

Traditional Christianity doesn't say a great deal about the beauty and uniqueness of planet earth. Indeed, verses such as these from the Psalms tend to give power to the view that we can just use the earth up like a resource as it is merely ancillary and incidental to the real deal that is God:

> Of old you laid the foundation of the earth, and the heavens are the work of your hands. They will perish, but you will remain; they will all wear out like a garment. You will change them like a robe, and they will pass away, but you are the same, and your years have no end.
> – Psalm 102:25–27

But there is a growing realisation and awareness of the truths of more ancient traditions and of those peoples that are still much more connected with the earth. Traditional communities often live a sustainable, environmentally friendly life, closely connected in a reverential and symbiotic relationship with planet earth. In turn, the earth communicates with them; such people respect our home planet as a living spirit.

New technology lets us see this in ever more compelling detail. There is growing evidence supporting James Lovelock's Gaia Theory, including compelling views of the earth from space. Check out this NASA video, which shows the seasonal cycle sped up – it shows the earth as if it were breathing: https://www.youtube.com/watch?v=hvMABV5JsTk

Experience this for yourself – connect with your home planet; connect deeply with this most precious jewel of God. Connect with the planet and you can connect directly and deeply with the spirit of God, for God's spirit is the marinade of the earth;

when you look upon this planet; when you let its power into your body and into your soul, you are letting in the power not of an inanimate rock, but of a living entity, the place that holds us and caresses us, that gives us food, water, air and shelter. The place made by the hand of God Himself. Be at one with your home. Treat it kindly, for it is the greatest jewel gifted to us by the Divine.

Contemplate:

- Does it surprise you how much disregard there has been in the past from the church towards the ecology of the planet?
- In what ways can you honour God by caring more for the earth? Make this part of your practice, your worship.

8

Life Music

Sing to him, sing praises to him; tell of all his wondrous
works!
– 1 Chronicles 16:9

Practice:

Today live your life in full knowledge that the everyday has
become the miraculous.

Know the grandeur of every breath, every action, everything
that comes your way. See the miracle in the smallest of places.

Feel the Divine's gift of your soul,
To be embodied.
Of your knowing of all that is in this day.
This miraculous day.
Listen to the music of life today.
Let the music burst forth from you.

Live this day as if it were your only one on this world.
Become the essence of the miracle in the heart of Divine Bliss.

On this day.

* * *

This practice dovetails beautifully with the 'Heaven Is Here!'
practice. Remember on this day that you are a spiritual being
temporarily experiencing life here on earth in human form. We
are here to experience and to love and to grow and develop.
But how much of our lives do we live in a trance? We are here

for a mere blip in eternity, so every moment is precious. Every moment is unique.

So feel everything as if it were music today. Move from the head to the heart and let the Divine burst forth from your heart centre and let the heart truly sing; let the music of the song of love feel the miraculous so deeply today. See the miraculous where previously you saw only the mundane.

Play the song from your heart, listen to the music of the earth, listen to the music of life, the music of the soul, the music of God.

Contemplate:

- Did you feel the living vibration and the wonder that is life on this planet?
- How much of this beauty is lost to those who do not let the scales fall from their eyes and truly experience this music of life?
- How can you sustain this beautiful experience in your life every day?

9

Be Free in Your Happiness

Therefore my heart is glad, and my whole being rejoices...
– Psalm 16:9

Practice:

Today I want you to be blissfully happy. Even if you don't feel it, then just pretend; BE! The more you fake it to begin with if you have to, you will find that before too long, you will find it to be more and more real.

Any negative thoughts that arise, simply cast them aside for the day.

Tell them to come back tomorrow, if they dare; tomorrow say the same to them. Eventually they will lose their power.

So for today, imagine or remember the happiest, most carefree person you've ever met.

Today you will be that person.

* * *

In my coaching practice, I once worked with a wonderful person who came from a privileged background, and who lived a very blessed life. When I first met her, the thing that most struck me was her smile. It shone from her, and it not only lit her face up, but it projected and radiated love and positivity. I just felt good in her presence.

But buried beneath the smile, there were a host of uncertainties and doubts. There were a multitude of Points of View; unresolved 'contractions' that got in the way of her really being able to radiate her glory fully out into the world. It was as if she were driving along with the handbrake still on.

We did an exercise whereby we asked those people who had known her a long time to give her feedback on her gifts, on her positive attributes (see 'Know Your Genius'). One of the qualities that came back more than most from the people who really knew her well was just how much fun she could be. This was part of her unconditioned nature, i.e. the real person, the real character.

The trouble is, she had lived for years with conditioning. This conditioning was people telling her that she needed to be more grounded and committed to achieving 'serious' things. The conditioning didn't manifest much to the outside observer, such was the strength of her inner personality – she still smiled and radiated happiness. However, internally, she felt as if something of the real 'her' was missing, and being held back.

So, through the coaching, we used a practice that was designed to let her step fully into her fun nature. Wow – what a difference just feeling as if she had the permission to do this made to her! She moved into her heart, lay aside any negative conditioning; she fully gave herself to the world; her light shone brighter and brighter. She infected everybody and everything around her with happiness. She was free and she flew like a bird.

So, even if you're not always jumping around with joy by nature, it doesn't matter. Just go for it in this practice – do it to the maximum just for one day. And if that day goes well, do it for a further day. And if that's good, do it for another one. Let that brake off. The more you practise something, the more it becomes built into the very fibre of your being as a habit.

When I do the school run with my daughters in the morning, it's often a time fraught with stress and panic – the tyranny of the clock, getting everything ready. So on the journey, some mornings, I will just start to laugh. My two-year-old daughter always finds this infectious and hilarious, and she too will begin to laugh uncontrollably. The laughter feeds off the laughter, then my older daughters can't help themselves, and before you know it, the car is a riot of laughter. Even though there was nothing outside of ourselves that instigated the laughter, we create the communion of mirth within and between us. When we laugh, nerves sent to the brain trigger electrical impulses to set off chemical reactions. These reactions release natural tranquilisers, pain relievers and endorphins. What a fabulous start to the day!

Can you see in this example how we created hilarity, joy and laughter from within ourselves? We usually make the mistake of thinking that happiness and joy is related somehow to our circumstances, that it is external to us, or 'exogenous'. Exogenous means that something is produced outside of a system or organism. Think about it – are we really that simple and un-complex an organism that we just grope around within circumstance, within life, dependent entirely upon factors outside of ourselves as to whether or not we experience happiness?

Certainly, we often just assume that if our circumstances get better, we will be happy. Indeed, this is a defining aspect of life for so many people – we pay thousands of pounds to acquire the latest gadgets; to go on the most faraway, exotic holidays; to develop a beautiful body; yet in all likelihood, our happiness quotient will not change at all as a result of altering our external circumstances.

Happiness has absolutely nothing to do with circumstances. Two people with identical circumstances can have vastly different levels of experiential happiness. If someone asks you, 'How are you doing today?' you might reply, 'Not bad under the circumstances.' But why do we assume that it's the circumstances that drive the happiness? Happiness is 'endogenous', i.e. produced within you. If it were produced externally, i.e. 'exogenously', then two people who had more or less the same external circumstances would have more or less the same degree of happiness in their lives. This we know not to be anywhere near the truth. Sustained happiness and joy never, ever comes from exogenous stimuli – it never ever comes from outside of ourselves. As my friend and 'virtual minister', Paul

John Roach of Unity Church, Fort Worth, Texas, says, 'Happiness is an inside job!'

This is another one of those realisations that is in itself 'psychoactive', i.e. the realisation alone of the truth, and the breaking of the trance of falsehood, can begin to re-program the brain to move in the direction of truth. So, in your daily life, be mindful of where happiness stems for you; be aware of the happiness that wells up in you from the smallest of things; make a habit of this awareness and amplify the feeling when it arises. Let your happiness free like in a child.

What a beautiful habit to bring into the world – HAPPINESS!

Contemplate:

- Happiness is flow. It flows in you, around you, between you and other people; when you give it out, it returns to you. Be conscious of the flow of happiness when you engage in this uplifting practice.
- Be aware of how you can increase the stock of happiness in you and in those with whom you connect.

10

Become Witness

I have been crucified with Christ. It is no longer I who live, but Christ who lives in me. And the life I now live in the flesh I live by faith in the Son of God, who loved me and gave himself for me.

– Galatians 2:20

Practice:

Sit comfortably.

Focus on your breathing.

Let all strain and stress just melt from your body.

Be aware of yourself.

Look around you.

Who is it that is seeing through these eyes?

Now be aware of feelings in your body. The arising of sensation.

Who is feeling these sensations?

Listen. Be aware of sound. Try to hear the sound furthest from you in this moment.

Who or what is aware of the sound?

Now turn within. Get a sense of yourself.

Your deepest 'self'.

Look within.

Can you sense where this 'you' is located?

Does it have a colour?

Does it have a shape?

Does it have any beginning or any end?

Is the real you located somewhere inside your head behind your eyes?

You may not be able to locate it in space at all.
Wherever or whatever it is, just feel it.
Get a sense of it.
Get a sense of the self.

Consider for a moment your external image that the world sees: you are your job; your relationships; your car; your house etc.
Notice this objective 'you' in form.

Now notice a second 'you'.
One 'you' is the self that you are looking at.
This is the objective self.
This is the self that can be seen; the observed.
The self that is the observer, the self that is looking, is the witnessing self.
This is the true self.
It cannot be seen.
It is not an object.
It is pure subject.
It is pure subjectivity – pure awareness.
This awareness cannot be seen or felt or heard. It has no form.
That means that it is the thing doing the observing, the real 'you' is beyond all of those things; it cannot be seen; it can only see.
Hence, it is pure awareness; pure consciousness; pure witness. It is the pure you.

As you rest in this place of pure witness, you will not see any objects in it.
If you see anything in there, they are just things that you are witnessing.
They are not what you really are.
Just rest and be.
Simply witness everything that arises from moment to moment.
Notice a sense of freedom.

Notice that you are no longer identified with the objects around you.

Say to yourself:

'I have sensations, but I am not my sensations',
'I have thoughts, but I am not my thoughts',
'I have memories but I am not my memories',
'I have feelings, but I am not my feelings',
'I have a body, but I am not my body',
'I have a job but I am not my job',
'I have a mind, but I am not my mind.'

So all you are is infinite freedom.

All of these objects are arising in your consciousness, but this is not what you are.

You are an infinite sense of witnessing spirit, pure awareness that has no objective form.

Rest for a while in the sense of liberation; of freedom; of infinite openness and transparency. Rest for a while in your true self; your core being; your core I-am-ness. Just witness; identify with nothing.

Know that nothing can hurt you; nothing can harm you; you are free of everything.

You are simply awareness.

You are pure witness, without any condemnation or judgement. Nobody can touch your awareness; nobody can take it away from you.

Rest for a while in this place.

* * *

Firstly, a reminder of what we mean by subject and object. In grammar, we define the object in a sentence as the entity that is acted upon by the subject. There is thus a distinction between subjects and objects in terms of action where we have a verb in a sentence. For example, 'I eat the banana.' Here, 'I' is the subject, and 'the banana' is the object. Or in the case of this phrase, 'I am basically my ego', the 'I' is the subject and 'my ego' is the object.

So, what do we mean by 'pure subjectivity' when we are thinking about ourselves? We are the victims of a case of mistaken identity. We have inadvertently identified with our small self, the outer self, the ego. It is embodied in a finite biological being that will live a while; it will have its ups and its downs, and will ultimately die.

What we are therefore attempting to do in this practice is to transcend your identity, to shift awareness away from the body and the mind and in so doing to anchor your 'being' in ultimate awareness. We therefore want you not to be identified with a false, narrow, partial, finite, limited self, but with a true, ultimate, real, spaceless, infinite and eternal self. Life trapped within the body holds a lot of suffering. Life awakened and liberated from this narrow view of self is free.

So, to liberate our self-identity from the narrow view of self, we need to understand the difference between subject and object. When we look at ourself, the 'we' or 'I' is the subject, and what we see as 'ourself' is the object. In this exercise, we continually go upwards in the 'subject' until we get to the subject that cannot be observed. As we move away and upwards like this, the subject of one level becomes the object of the subject at the next, higher level.

For example, if we say, 'I' am observing the 'me', then 'I' is the subject, and 'me' is the object. If we move up a level, we make the 'I' the object, and the person who is aware of the 'I' is now the subject. We can continue to do this, moving up and away from the object until the object loses all 'objectivity'. When the 'I' becomes merely the observer, and not the observed, to the point where we cannot see the 'I', where it loses all form, then we have reached the self that is the true self. Hence, it is pure 'subjectivity' as it cannot be seen. It is pure awareness, pure consciousness.

In Luke 4:18 (NIV), Jesus said, 'The Spirit of the Lord is on me, because he has anointed me to proclaim good news to the poor. He has sent me to proclaim freedom for the prisoners and recovery of sight for the blind, to set the oppressed free...' This practice, when undertaken in alignment with the Spirit of God, will set you free from the oppression of 'self'. It will free you from the cage of the ego.

This may be the first time that you have become fully conscious of the deepest self; it is certainly something that is little understood in traditional Western religion. It is central to mending the relationship between us and God, and as such, many of the practices in this book will reinforce this truth of who we really are. We want to get you plugged into that awareness of the very essence of your being, the awareness of yourself as an eternal spirit, undivided from God who is ultimate Divine Spirit. If you're going to get identified with something, then you couldn't do much better than identify with the ultimate reality, which is Spirit itself!

Indeed, as you contemplate this over the next few days and weeks, you will come to recognise that the pure, formless, un-manifest 'I-am-ness' can become one with every thing that is being witnessed, every objective thing. This is the essence of non-dual consciousness. It is the union of emptiness and form.

This results in an absolute all-embracing, all-permeating reality. However, even this is merely a dualistic description and is ultimately not absolutely true. The reality can only actually be known by directly experiencing it; directly awakening to it. Reading about it on this page isn't enough. It has to be viscerally known through personal experience. All words are merely an abstraction of reality. The person who reads these words without any experience might as well be reading an airport novel. The person who knows through experience, however, is suddenly transformed and this is what some people call an 'awakening' experience. It is when ultimate reality becomes directly and personally realised.

Maybe the closest analogy we can use to explain experience versus description is this: imagine that you have never eaten an apple. Somebody describes to you what an apple tastes like. She might say that it is crispy on the outside and that she gets a sharp, tangy, juicy taste and sensation. However, unless you actually eat an apple for yourself, you will never get anywhere near actually experiencing the reality of the taste and the texture of the apple. Even once you have finished the apple, and you are simply remembering what the tasting experience of eating the apple is like, this in itself isn't even the reality of the apple because it's merely a memory; it isn't the visceral present reality of knowing what eating the apple is like in the moment.

Ultimate reality, on the other hand, is empty of anything we could actually say about it. The true nature of reality is beyond words, beyond description. As with the apple, any words we use to describe ultimate reality will inevitably fall so far short of the thing we're trying to describe as to be close to useless.

It is very similar to the plot of the movie, *The Matrix*. We spend our lives going about our daily business thinking that we're in the real world. Well, it is a real world in a sense; it is a world of form, but form that has been given meaning through our own consciousness. Lying beyond and within all of what we think of as the real world is the world of ultimate reality. When we awaken to this formless realm of 'what is', we open the window of the heart to the true meeting place of us and God. We no longer experience the duality of the 'us' and our narrow-minded, limited notion of 'God'. When we enter into the realm of formlessness, Spirit then truly becomes 'one', and all notions of 'self' melt away. So, too, does judgement. There is nothing left to judge; all that is left is *witness*.

Contemplate:

- Does this help you to find a path to non-judgement of yourself and of others?
- Can you see that the more we are trapped in and identified with the world of the ego-driven self and the world of form, the more we have a tendency to judge? The more we awaken to our true nature, the more judgement merely melts away.
- When you discover that your true nature is simply awareness, do you feel closer to yourself and to God?
- Jesus said he came to set us free. Reflect how this practice helps to transform that truth from mere words to a reality in your day-to-day existence.

11

I Let Spirit Bless My Time

But do not overlook this one fact, beloved, that with the Lord one day is as a thousand years, and a thousand years as one day.
– 2 Peter 3:8

Practice:
As you get up in the morning, affirm:

I value every moment.

I am living in each moment, for only the present is real.

I am ready in every moment to be blessed, and for the works of my hands and the words of my mouth to be blessed.

Each moment of my life is divine, because it is a gift from God.

When I rise in the morning, I am excited, I greet the day in anticipation, because I know with certainty that I let God into every minute of this day.

Anticipation is the energy that allows me to spring out of bed ready to greet the new day!

I crave the experience of the unexpected, and anticipation works through my heart to increase my vibration, working like a magnet to pull good to me.

When I share my anticipation with others, they too are

energised, multiplying the joy that we all experience.

I look forward to the activities that this day holds, knowing that there is something wonderful about to happen, because I know that God works through the things that I planned and the things that I didn't plan.

With joy and expectation, I fully let God into the space that we call 'time'.

Centring my awareness on God, I recognise that I have enough time to accomplish more than I ever dreamed.

I recognise that there is opportunity to fulfil my mission in the world in every moment.

* * *

Those of us who are spiritually aware can sometimes have a tendency to be a little disorganised and chaotic. We can then allow this prism of chaos to take over our lives; we let the clutter of our diaries, and the stress that it induces, also create clutter in our heads. This cannot help us to still ourselves and create space for Spirit to move. Hence the importance of including this practice which brings practical and spiritual discernment and order to our daily life.

If you still think that there's not enough time in the day, just try this: set your watch to two minutes and watch it as it counts the time. Don't do anything else. Just watch the time tick by. Lasts an eternity, eh? You have around 500 of these episodes every day at your disposal. So, use them wisely. As well as the affirmations above, try these techniques:

- Set your mission and goals (see the chapters 'Know Your Genius' and 'Live Your Mission' for more detail).

- Set your objectives; link your objectives to the goals. Remember that the mission and goals are your 'what'; the objectives are the 'how'.
- Ensure that these objectives are SMART, i.e.
  - Specific
  - Measurable
  - Achievable
  - Realistic
  - Time-framed
- Every day, transfer relevant tasks from these objectives into your daily diary. Remember, this is your best attempt to fulfil God's mission in your life for this day. However, if unexpected things turn up, and things move around, then say to yourself, 'This is by Divine design.' Say to yourself, 'I wonder who I am supposed to meet here', or 'This seemingly random event was guided by the Angels.' Things will be taken care of in the right time – in God's time. Be open to the flow – it's being taken care of. Let God's good come to YOU!
- Do not multitask. Studies have shown that nobody is really able to multitask in any event. All you are really doing is flitting rapidly between one task and another. That way, things take twice as long and they are done in a less effective manner.
- Get order, overview and control in your work environment; ensure that only the thing you want to do at that time is in front of you – in fact, put everything else out of your sight line and reach.
- Try doing each task deliberately slowly. Paradoxically, it will help things speed up. Time in the sphere of the mind is effectively elastic. As well as psychological time, we have a spiritual time as shown in the Bible verse above. So you can see that for all practical purposes, your notion of time may be at fault, not the seeming fact that you don't

have enough of it!

- Be fully present to the things that you are doing in the moment.
- Be grateful for the blessings you have and the tasks you've been blessed with doing.
- Know that God is in charge; ask God to bless your 'to do' lists.
- Enjoy carrying out each indicated action.
- Let Go and Let God! Know that God is working behind the scenes, making arrangements with the Angels on your behalf, preparing the way.
- Be aware of the things that are in your circle of interest/ concern versus your circle of influence, i.e. the things that are in your interest/concern are really big and wide – everything that is of concern to you in any way, or in which you hold an interest. Can you control all of these things? Do you have any influence over all of them? Be honest – probably not! So, draw a circle and write down everything in the circle of influence, i.e. the things that you yourself can do to change things; then draw a wider circle outside the circle of influence. This is your circle of interest, or circle of concern. Write down all of the things that are of interest and of concern to you, but over which you have little or no influence. For these issues, just hold them up to God – Let Go and Let God. Let yourself off the hook and let God work on your behalf!
- Surrender your belief that you have to control everything. If you try to hold on to everything, then you're effectively restricting the power of Spirit to flow into all of these areas. Let Spirit work on your behalf! Release the Angels to go and work for your higher good. When you do this, you'll find that little miracles and coincidences happen all over the place; it's as if you have a spiritual team setting things up for you and working on your affairs.

- You only have a certain amount of human energy. Use it for the things that are yours to do; give the rest up to the infinite power and energy of Spirit...or other people for whom those things are theirs to do.
- As a rough rule of thumb, therefore, work on the little things and let Spirit take care of the bigger picture.
- If you begin to feel the pressure of constraints building, just feel into 'love' (see 'Love and Fear'). Relax into what you are doing with love flowing; it's often fear that drives us to try to multitask. If you find this tricky, then do the joyful, easy task first. Get into the flow of love; then once you're in the flow, move on to the seemingly more challenging task, but with the same spirit of love. It will flow!
- When your mind is aligned with God, so too will events in your life begin to line up. Thank God for those things; become increasingly aware of the Angels working on your behalf.

Affirm:

(with the in-breath) I relax my mind;
(with the out-breath) God blesses my time.

Say this over a few times.
Say this when you feel the need to surrender.

Contemplate:

- When you align with your higher purpose and give to God what is His and do what is yours to do, can you feel Spirit working in you and blessing your calendar?
- How liberating does it feel when you Let Go and Let God?
- Think over your entire life. If you apply this methodology, how much more time will you effectively liberate to live out your purpose here on earth?

12

Acceptance and Non-Judgement

Why do you pass judgement on your brother? Or you, why do you despise your brother? For we will all stand before the judgement seat of God; for it is written, 'As I live, says the Lord, every knee shall bow to me, and every tongue shall confess to God.' So then each of us will give an account of himself to God. Therefore let us not pass judgement on one another any longer, but rather decide never to put a stumbling block or hindrance in the way of a brother.
– Romans 14:10–13

Judge not, that you be not judged. For with the judgement you pronounce you will be judged, and with the measure you use it will be measured to you. Why do you see the speck that is in your brother's eye, but do not notice the log that is in your own eye? Or how can you say to your brother, 'Let me take the speck out of your eye', when there is the log in your own eye? You hypocrite, first take the log out of your own eye, and then you will see clearly to take the speck out of your brother's eye.
– Matthew 7:1–5

Practice:
Say this beautiful affirmation to yourself:

'I accept everyone I know and everyone I encounter every day, just as they are.'

Then, as the day unfolds, be aware of any moments in which feelings of judgement arise. If you find yourself being critical of others or judging them, simply say to yourself:

'They are [fill in the judgement] just like me',
e.g. 'That man is arrogant, just like me.'

This is one of the most effective and powerful of all practices. So much of our life is lived in judgement of others. Like non-forgiveness, this often has more of a deleterious effect on ourselves than it has on the other people.

Judgement is something that often stems from our ego's desire to put itself at the heart of everything. This can take many forms. Traditionally, we think of the ego as a person's self-esteem or self-importance. Going deeper, it is the part of the mind that mediates between the conscious and the unconscious and is responsible for protection, self-preservation, and a sense of personal identity.

The ego is also involved in putting itself at the centre of things when it comes to our judgement or criticism of others. We will look at this in more detail in our practice on 'Shadow Work' in a later chapter. For now, here is a brief explanation of the 'shadow' and how we need to understand it for the purposes of this practice.

Carl Jung described the shadow as the unknown or hidden dark side of our personality. According to Jung, the shadow, or the part of us that we don't want to acknowledge, that we want to keep hidden, is prone to psychological projection. Thus a potential personal inferiority is 'projected' away from ourselves and appears in our consciousness as a perceived moral or character deficiency in someone else. Put simply, we don't like this aspect of ourselves, so the ego finds ways of pinning it upon somebody else.

So, when you criticise or judge others, just pause a little and think into the thing that you are criticising. As the ego always wants to draw attention back to 'self', there's a remarkable fact that the things we most tend to criticise are indeed our very own character traits that we want to disavow and keep hidden. Our ego, however, rather than keeping them hidden in the shadow, tends to manifest these traits through judgement of others.

Therefore, be very aware of what you are criticising. If you are open and honest with your reflections, you will often recognise that it is an aspect of yourself. Thus by saying to yourself, 'just like me', you are honestly bringing the projected judgement back from the 'third person' (the other) to the 'first person' (yourself).

The other negative effect of this projection and judgement of others is that it encourages a sense of separation. The act of judging and looking disparagingly at others pushes them away from us. It promulgates the notion of distance between us and other people. There is the 'us' and there is the 'other'. By saying 'just like me', we shatter the divide which separates us from the person we are criticising. We are therefore bringing ourselves into holistic healing with the whole; we are furthermore resolving the artificial sense of separation that ignites fear into our consciousness.

Hence this practice shines love both as a healing remedy on ourselves, onto relationships and onto the communion of humankind as a whole.

Contemplate:

- When you find yourself criticising others, consider whether what you're looking at are actually your own character traits that you'd rather you didn't have.
- Think on the power of three simple words – 'just like me'. How much healing can spring from such a short, simple phrase?
- We probably all judge others multiple times every day. Get into a habit, therefore, of saying 'just like me' several times a day, when the judgemental situation arises. Keep it in

the forefront of your mind. It will often make you smile to yourself internally when you say it; if this happens, then you are removing the power from the judgement; you are dissolving the negative with a smile or a chuckle.

13

Play!

And the streets of the city shall be full of boys and girls playing in its streets.
– Zechariah 8:5

Practice:

If you have children in your life, then PLAY!

Even if you don't, you don't need them as an excuse, so still just PLAY!

Do something silly today,
Do it in any way,
Don't let your day be grey,
Splay, stray, sway, pray, flay, neigh,
Do whatever,
Come what may,
Just PLAY!!!

When I first read the New Testament cover to cover, the thing that most struck me was how rounded a human being Jesus was. Within this, it struck me that he was really very radical and rebellious. This reality is so far removed from the traditional image of Jesus as being rather melancholy and glum, or meek and mild.

Indeed, the Gospels paint a picture of a fully developed, charismatic personality. He loved children. In Mark 10:16, it says that Jesus took some children in his arms and blessed them. Can you imagine Jesus being anything other than bright, beautiful and friendly with the little ones?

In Luke 6:21 (NLT), Jesus says, 'God blesses you who weep

now, for in due time you will laugh.' So we see that laughter and the full panoply of human emotion was in Jesus' consciousness.

The very fact that we humans have a sense of humour indicates that God does, too, for we are made in His image. When we laugh, when we play, we strengthen the purity and the passion that is in our heart of love. If you lose yourself fully to laughter and to play, especially with children, it opens the heart to the fun and the beauty and the purity that is at the core of 'what is' – connection with those around you, connection that is centred in LOVE!

Contemplate:

- Have you ever mistakenly thought that the spiritual life must be one of seriousness and po-faced disapproval?
- How did it feel to open your heart and lose yourself in play?
- Did you manage to just be a little bit (or very!) silly?
- Can you see that as embodied spirits, we need to open ourselves to every aspect of love, of humanity, in order to experience the full glory of God's expression in us?
- Did opening the window of the heart through play help your spiritual walk today?

14

Pure Seeing; Pure Being

For just as the body is one and has many members, and all the members of the body, though many, are one body, so it is with Christ. For in one Spirit we were all baptized into one body – Jews or Greeks, slaves or free – and all were made to drink of one Spirit. For the body does not consist of one member but of many. If the foot should say, 'Because I am not a hand, I do not belong to the body', that would not make it any less a part of the body. And if the ear should say, 'Because I am not an eye, I do not belong to the body', that would not make it any less a part of the body.
– 1 Corinthians 12:12–16

All that is necessary to awaken to yourself as the radiant emptiness of spirit is to stop seeking something more or better or different, and to turn your attention inward to the awake silence that you are.
– Adyashanti

Practice:

Close your eyes.

Listen. Just listen.

What can you hear?

Does it take any effort to be able to hear the sounds in the room? The sounds outside the window?

Is there any time delay between the sounds arising and your hearing the sounds?

Do you need to think in order to hear the sounds?

So would it be true to say that hearing requires no effort and no thought, and that there is no time delay in the hearing?

Who or what is aware of the sounds arising in this moment?
Just be that which is listening right now. Relax into that.

Keeping your eyes closed, feel.
Just feel.
What can you feel?
Can you feel the weight of your back in the chair?
Can you feel the air upon your face?
Does it take any effort to be able to feel these things?
Is there any time delay between your body feeling things and being aware of feelings?
Do you need to think in order to feel?
So would it be true to say that feeling requires no effort and no thought, and that there is no time delay in the feeling?
Who or what is aware of the feelings arising in this moment?
Just be that which is feeling right now. Relax into that.

Now gently open your eyes.
See. Look out of the window.
What can you see?
Can you see any movement of tree branches in the wind?
Can you see any people moving around or birds in flight?
Does it take any effort to be able to see these things?
Is there any time delay between the movement and your awareness of the movement?
Do you need to think in order to see?
So would it be true to say that seeing requires no effort and no thought, and that there is no time delay in the seeing?
Who or what is aware of the things that you can see in this moment?
Just be that which is seeing right now.

Now close your eyes.
Can you separate this moment from all other moments? Can

you experience this moment without thinking about any other moment?

Rest as that which is aware.

Who is aware of seeing, of hearing and of feeling?

If you answer, 'me', or 'I', or 'my brain', then ask yourself the question, 'Who or what is aware of any of these things?' Go deeper. Who or what is aware of the 'I'?

Keep on going deeper; go on further and further back until you can see no 'I'; just the pure consciousness that is aware of the 'I'. Go back until you cannot see the awareness that is aware.

Now you have discovered the pure awareness that resides at the heart of who you are. This is the pure 'see-er', the pure 'I-am-ness'. This is truly who you are.

Now rest in that awareness. Rest in that pure 'self'.

Ask yourself the question, 'What shape does this pure "self" have?'

Does it have any colour?

Does it have any beginning or any end?

Does it elicit any feeling?

Does it make any sound?

Just continue to sink deeper into pure being. Relax and enjoy it; this is a beautiful place to be.

* * *

This is a remarkable practice. It sits at the root of what Ken Wilber describes as 'waking up'. We use a similar methodology in Awakening Coaching as one of the key, fundamental practices.

Its importance lies in the realisation that you are more than your physical body. It might be the first time in your life that you have discovered your true nature. It lies at the heart of what many call 'enlightenment'. I prefer simply to call it 'awakening', as it is a verb – it is something that happens to us in the moment. Being awake cannot exist in the future and it cannot exist in the past; it is firmly rooted in the present moment. Furthermore, waking up to one's true nature doesn't endow us with superhuman powers; hence, the term 'enlightenment' can be misleading, as it is so loaded with assumptions and false hope.

Awakening simply means that, in any given moment, we can be aware of our true nature. Our true nature as a spirit, living life embodied with human characteristics; our true nature that, deep down, is just pure awareness. That is who we are. We are aware; we are awake to 'what is'. This means that instead of our head being filled with the endless churning of thought, of thinking about concepts, plans, ideas, the future and the past, we are just present to what is around us right here and right now.

From this point, as we awaken to our true nature, we can begin to truly explore and to live in full consciousness of who we are, of our relationship with God, of our relationship with other people, indeed, of our relationship with the entire manifest Universe.

This really is the starting point of everything. So much of Western religion is connected with understanding the nature of God; so little is understood about who WE truly are. That's why the relationship often fails between us and God – we only truly focus on one half of the relationship. When we immerse ourselves, however, in both the nature of our own being and the nature of the being of 'what is', then we can experience true, expansive, creative freedom within the spaciousness of Spirit.

Contemplate:

- Did you experience a sudden rush of consciousness, of a door opening, or of a light being switched on?
- How did this practice affect you?
- In the days and the weeks following this practice, how has it shifted your awareness of who you are, your place in the world, and your relationship with God?

- When you do this practice, do you feel the spaciousness at the heart of who you are?
- The awareness doing the listening or seeing or feeling is not really a 'thing'; it's pure consciousness. So if you are in essence 'no-thing', and everything else and everybody else is 'no-thing', then what separates nothing from nothing? Answer: Nothing! Reflect therefore on how this practice enables you to sense the lack of separateness between all things; the essential unity that lies at the heart of all being.

15

Go with the Flow

Whoever believes in me, as the Scripture has said, 'Out of his heart will flow rivers of living water.'
– John 7:38

Practice:

Row, row, row the boat,
Gently down the stream…

I align with the plan of God in my life,
I let Spirit in to my life as my guide.

I surrender fully to the will of the Universe,
I recognise that I am one with the Universe,
I know that I AM the Universe.

As I align with the Divine,
All thoughts of limitation and of lack dissolve away,
Like puffs of cloud on the wind.

I now know that separation from God
Is a false thought.

I know and affirm that as Spirit flows through me,
All I need to do is to rest in the knowledge that I am an
essential part of the whole,
That if I didn't exist, or if I denied the truth of my being,
Then the whole would no longer be whole.

I now offer no resistance,
I don't even just 'go with the flow',
I AM the flow.

* * *

When we struggle with a project or a desire, and the doors keep on slamming on us and we keep on getting knocked back, just remember that little nursery rhyme about rowing down the stream. It certainly isn't, '*Row, row, row your boat furiously against the tide...*'

How much easier is it if we let the canoe drift along with the stream? Or if we're playing tennis and we hit the perfect shot, connecting the racquet with the ball right in the centre of the sweet spot? The ball flies, and we don't feel anything – it's as if we've had to make no effort, yet the results are remarkable.

So at times when you feel as if it's all just struggle, say the above affirmation to yourself. Feel into the will of Spirit. Relax and let God take the effort from you. Still do what is yours to do, but separate the tasks – you do your work, and let God do His!

When you fully align with the will of God, then you enter into a 'flow state'. This is an immensely powerful state of being where you can accomplish great things in a relatively short space of time. The more you practise this way of being, the more you can enter into these flow states. They can be truly transformative.

Contemplate:
- Look back in your life at the things that took an incredible amount of energy and that felt like an overwhelming task/chore, where obstacles kept on arising. Do you think in retrospect that you were aligned with the will of God?
- Think of times when you've worked hard and long, but it felt like no effort or stress at all. Recognise that you were aligned with the flow.

Chapter 15

- Think about things that might have been an effort, but strange coincidences kept on occurring that helped you on your way; things fell into place as if guided by a mysterious hand – again, do you think that you were aligned with the will of God? Can you see what the Angels were setting up in advance for you?

- Be aware of struggle – discern the difference between good, productive struggle that feels like 'flow', and unproductive struggle that doesn't bring good into your life or the lives of those around you.

16

Wisdom

If any of you lacks wisdom, let him ask God, who gives generously to all without reproach, and it will be given him.
– James 1:5

Blessed is the one who finds wisdom, and the one who gets understanding, for the gain from her is better than gain from silver and her profit better than gold. She is more precious than jewels, and nothing you desire can compare with her. Long life is in her right hand; in her left hand are riches and honour. Her ways are ways of pleasantness, and all her paths are peace.
– Proverbs 3:13–17

Yesterday I was clever, so I wanted to change the world. Today I am wise, so I am changing myself.
– Rumi

Practice:
If you find yourself struggling with a problem, not knowing which path to take, then lay aside your struggles.
Just STOP!

Stop thinking,
Stop analysing,
Stop writing lists,
Stop scoring alternatives.

Move away from the head,
Consciously move down to the heart centre.

Connect with the Spirit within,
Ask Spirit to be your way-shower,
Humble yourself before God and move away from your own
intellect, your own strength.

Now, when the time is right – it may be now, it may be tomorrow,
it may be in a few days – ask Spirit to reveal the answer to you
in your heart centre.
Again, move away from the head and go inside to find the
truth.

Feel into the right path, feel into the certainty of the right
direction.
Feel into the deepest wisdom, from the depths of Spirit,
Feel the certainty of the path of Truth.
Let love be your guide, banish any fear.

Know the truth, let its light fill your body and your soul with
The certainty of the Spirit within.

* * *

In today's scientific world, we see at a certain level of
consciousness a drive to separate knowledge into its constituent
parts – a reductive materialism that seeks to derive greater and
deeper knowledge from an increasingly narrow field of study.
Thus we are becoming ever more specialised and ever less
integrated. Wisdom, on the other hand, appears to be a lost art.
Indeed, it seems as if it is a word that is falling out of favour,
out of fashion. The word 'wisdom' appears over 200 times in the
Bible. How often do you hear the word said in common usage
nowadays? Rarely?

No degree of knowledge and study, or accumulation of facts,
can produce wisdom. Wisdom is distinct from knowledge,

therefore cannot be replaced by it. Information, and the accumulated knowledge of facts, is increasing globally at an exponential rate, driven by population growth, the broadening base of education and scientific endeavour, and the connectedness that is brought about by computerised networks. However, information is by its very nature limited by virtue of the fact that you could, theoretically, catalogue and count it. Conversely, we cannot count wisdom, so in some respects, it is infinite; it is deeper and it works on a more metaphysical plane.

Wisdom is defined often as the ability to use knowledge and experience to make good decisions and judgements. But it is so much more than the sum of knowledge and experience. The infinite nature of wisdom is derived from its intrinsically holistic nature. You could theoretically feed enormous amounts of data related to experience and knowledge into a computer and ask it via algorithms to churn out a response to a situation. Would this make it wise? Absolutely not! If we reduce knowledge and experience down to raw data, we can never experience the beauty of the holons within which wisdom sits. Intellect and knowledge can never point to the whole, for it is merely a two-dimensional and limited slice of the human condition.

This is why we need to turn within, to deeper dimensions of 'self', in order to seek wisdom. And when we turn within, we turn to our own Christ Nature, the indwelling Kingdom of God, for true guidance. We seek at all levels – the human nature where we use our God-given intellect and often hard-earned life experience, combined with the supernatural guidance of Spirit. And we wait. We combine head and heart until the two align with Spirit. When we open ourselves up and humble ourselves before God, knowing that only He is truly wise, then we are on the path to letting wisdom shape our lives.

Contemplate:

- How does it feel to surrender and to let go, to humble yourself before God?
- How easy is it to move away from a left-brained, analysis-driven approach?
- Have you ever used the latter methodology, but felt in your heart that you had got it wrong? How did it feel?
- Scientists have discovered neurons in the heart and in the gut; some dispute the fact that we can therefore think with these organs, but it may indicate why we get feelings such as 'gut feel', and 'feelings of the heart'. Practise moving down from the head and feeling into the heart and gut when it comes to decisions. When you do this, what results do you get in your day-to-day life?

17

Let Nature Be Your Guide

For what can be known about God is plain to them, because God has shown it to them. For his invisible attributes, namely, his eternal power and divine nature, have been clearly perceived, ever since the creation of the world, in the things that have been made.
– Romans 1:19–20

You carry Mother Earth within you. She is not outside of you. Mother Earth is not just your environment. In that insight of inter-being, it is possible to have real communication with the Earth, which is the highest form of prayer.
– Thich Nhat Hanh

Practice:

Take a walk alone in the woods.

Walk until your intuition tells you to stop by a particular tree.

Stand for a while looking in detail at the tree – its solidity; how it sinks down into the earth; feel the texture of the bark; the shape of the branches and how they divide.

Get to know the tree. Introduce yourself. Ask the tree some questions; listen with your intuitive ear for the answers.

Now just sit among the trees.

Hear the trees speak to you.

Feel the wisdom of time.

Let their spirit mingle with yours.

Take your time; become one with the forest.

Before you leave, honour the living forest by giving a bow.

* * *

Chapter 17

I have practised this from time to time over the years. I am always staggered at how much living personality is exuded by the trees. They don't communicate as we do; obviously there is no language, but you can feel their life, their wisdom.

I was once trekking in Patagonia, in a remote forest-scape. I sat for a while with my legs dangling over a low inland cliff. The weak Patagonian sunshine came out for a while to greet me and I lay back, dozing for some time.

I awoke with a start, as I sensed something near me. Looking round, I saw a large, grey fox standing, staring at me. Soon the fox ambled off, leaving me all alone once more. In this deep, lost forest, I had this overwhelming feeling of something else; something alive. As I wandered through the trees, I was overcome with the sense of the living spirit of the forest. The trees were huge here, probably some 50 metres high. I felt as if they were looking at me. I felt them welcoming me, but letting me know that I was just a visitor; that this was their domain.

The longer I spent in the forest, the more the secrets and timelessness of the place manifested. Somehow, even many years on, I feel changed for the experience. I felt as if I had communed with mother earth herself. I acknowledge that we are just passing through. The sacred nature of the planet is eternal. When we connect directly with the earth, we are connecting with the Divine.

Contemplate:

- When you connect with God through nature, directly and without words or doctrine, or structure, feel into the presence of 'What Is'. Without using words, using only your intuition, consider how this feels to you.
- How does it touch your heart?
- How does it change you?
- What can you take back to your regular life?

18

Shadow Work

The light shines in the darkness, and the darkness has not overcome it.
– John 1:5

Note that we use the word 'reactive' in this practice. This is similar to the phrase 'acting out', i.e. when we react externally and negatively to impulse, in contrast to bearing and managing the impulse internally.

Practice:

Make sure that you are in a comfortable place.

You could be lying down, you could be sitting.

Close your eyes.

Become more aware of your breathing.

Let your belly soften.

Be aware of the inhale and the exhale of your breath.

As you continue to let your body soften, bring to mind a situation in which you were reactive, when you reacted negatively.

It could have been to another person; it could have been to a situation.

It could have been today.

It could have been last week.

If you don't remember, just picture how you are when you are reactive.

Visualise yourself being reactive.

Let it be vivid.

See where you are; your body position. Are you leaning forward?

What are you doing with your arms and your hands?

Chapter 18

What is your body position relative to that of others in your vicinity?

What are you saying?

Is your jaw tense?

Is your voice raised?

Are you perspiring?

Is your heartbeat raised?

Whatever it is, hold this in your consciousness, even as you continue to let yourself breathe.

Continue to be aware of each inhale, each exhale, your belly getting softer.

Imagine now that you are moving closer to this reactive 'you'.

They look just like you but you have never seen yourself looking this way before. You sense a heightened level of negative energy and fear.

The reactive you is tighter, more contracted.

There's a palpable sense of tension.

Without judging or criticising, move closer.

Imagine looking dispassionately into the face of the reactive you.

You are looking straight into your own eyes.

Your breathing is calm and steady.

You are letting yourself feel this one.

Let your present state of awareness dissolve away.

You now are really feeling the reactive version of you.

Look deeper into your own eyes.

Now visualise the reactive 'you' before you as a child.

A very upset child.

Hurt, lost, fearful.

This is the little you as a five-year-old child.

Now imagine that you are bringing this little child closer to you.

You're letting this five-year-old version of yourself come closer to your heart.

Imagine bringing this hurt and fearful 'you' into your heart.

You are not telling your five-year-old self to be quiet or to stop what they are doing.

You are simply opening yourself to them.

The narrative that triggered the hurt and the upset doesn't matter, it isn't important.

You are simply feeling into the heart of the little child that was once you.

You are letting your emotional receptivity tune into them.

Now get even closer.

You are now feeling emotion at one with the little child.

Now sense in your body where this lodges most.

Can you feel a contraction, or a sense of unease?

It could be in your throat or your heart, or your belly or your back.

Just try and find the contraction.

Feel into the body. Don't look higher than the neck or lower than the waist.

Just acknowledge the contraction, the unease, and after a few moments, gently let it go.

Now look back at the little child. Give him or her a hug. Hold the child tight in an embrace.

And as you continue to hold the child tight, continue to let your feelings merge.

Hold that one just for a moment or two.

Just continue to cultivate intimacy with this very hurt aspect of yourself.

Don't try to get this other 'you' to soften or to change; just be with it, as you would be with an upset child.

Be an assertive holder of the space.

Now begin to feel more of a distance between the two 'yous'.
Become gradually more aware of yourself.
Become more aware of your breathing.
Move back now into your present body.

Now be fully back in the room in the now in your body. Wiggle
your fingers, move your feet, but continue to maintain a deep
sense of empathy and caring for the part of you that is reactive.

* * *

Know that this does not mean that you will never be 'reactive'
again, but you have increased the odds that the next time, you
might approach things a little differently.

Every one of us has shadow elements, and one of the signs
of this is 'reactivity'. This is part of our human condition. This
practice is a simple first step in consciously recognising shadow
as it arises, and dealing with it.

We touch on 'shadow' in several chapters of this book, such
is its importance in personal and spiritual growth. Simply put,
shadow is whatever we're keeping in the dark about ourselves.
They are the aspects that we've disowned about ourselves,
or pushed to one side and not acknowledged. Our tendency
is to treat the reactive self in the third person – we treat it as
something other than a part of us. The aim of this exercise is to
fully open up to it and acknowledge that the reactivity within us
is indeed part of us.

By breaking the tendency to disavow and disown this part
of us, we give ourselves the opportunity to open up to the
knowledge and the reality of who we are and in so doing begin
to construct the pathway to healing.

Our conditioning, i.e. the way we may have changed or

reacted to events and situations in our life, may produce shadow. For example, if we have reacted to anger in situations in the past, then we may have an aversion to anger which we have pushed into the shadows. It may also simply manifest as a natural part of what makes us who we are. We are not trying to analyse or judge or criticise here. Whatever has promulgated the shadow elements within us isn't the point. This is why we can pretty much ignore the backstory, the narrative. The point is that we all have this shadow self, but now we are able to recognise it and therefore know how to integrate it in a healthy fashion into our holistic sense of being, of self.

When you know your shadow and become intimate with all that you are, you can begin to integrate all aspects of your being in your journey through life. If you remain aware only of the positive elements, then any growth tends not to be maintained and sustained so well. Understanding your shadow and knowing how to deal with it produces a much more healthy environment in which to incorporate new understanding, which in turn leads to growth. By becoming intimate with all that we are, the light and the shadow, we can begin to transform our lives.

Any spiritual work must therefore entail exposure to and understanding of the things that we normally tend to deny about ourselves. If we only focus on finding our goodness and try not to acknowledge feelings of shame, guilt, jealousy, greed, competition, lust and aggression, then we are denying a part of ourselves; we resist bringing our fullest 'self' to the table.

When we ignore our shadow self, we are repressing it. How many times have you tried to enter a quiet place, maybe in prayer or in meditation, but as soon as you shut your eyes, these shadow thoughts and desires will not go away. When we consciously acknowledge the shadow, we break the spell that it holds over us. Its dominion is diminished. We shift from projecting the shadow side of ourselves from our inner consciousness onto the outside world, and move to integrate it into wholeness; we bring it out of the shadows, and acknowledge it.

If we only acknowledge a partial picture of ourselves, we create separation. When we find ways of re-establishing the totality of ourselves as a holistic being, we dissolve separation and therefore it becomes so much more difficult to project our shadow from the inner to the outer as the separation between inner and outer no longer exists. We are therefore able to re-establish a healthy foundation upon which to build and to grow.

Lastly, note that we should always try to meet the shadow in a safe and loving way. There should be no self-condemnation. This is a courageous and important step towards healing and self-love and you should only undertake this practice when you are feeling centred and calm. Never undertake this practice when you are in a state of reactivity in the moment.

Contemplate:

- What aspects of your whole self did this practice reveal?
- Feel into how you can incorporate regular shadow work within your spiritual practice and meditation.

19

The Golden Shadow

Therefore do not throw away your confidence, which has a great reward.
– Hebrews 10:35

Practice:

Make a list of all the people that you find truly great and that you admire.

Write down the qualities that you appreciate the most in these people.

What you have is a likely list of your own projected positive material that you have been hiding in the shadows.

The people you have identified may well have these qualities, but while you might be a great fan of these people, other people are not, or they don't see the qualities.

So what is the difference in perception between you who appreciate those people and others who do not?

You see the other person as great because you subconsciously see your shadow positive qualities in that other person. Other people don't see it because they do not possess those qualities.

You are increasing that person's greatness by projecting your greatness onto them at the same time as you are losing or giving away your greatness by projecting it away from yourself.

You can start to reclaim this greatness back to yourself by practising the 3-2-1 process:

3: Identify the projected material, the things you excessively love about that person. So, write a list of all of the things that you really like about that person (things seen in them, i.e. third person).

Chapter 19

2: Face it, talk to it as a second person. Return to your list and say out loud, for example: 'I really like you because you are charismatic'; 'I love the way you openly communicate with me.'

1: Talk as it, i.e. in the first person. So, for example, you may say, 'I am a charismatic person'; 'I am good at openly communicating with other people.'

Then *be* it; be the quality, thus re-owning the quality.

Talk as one who truly owns this quality – fully integrate it back into your person.

Do this for a few minutes each day for a few days. At the end of each day, think about the most positively impactful people you've met that day and practise the 3-2-1 process.

This will begin to clean up your golden shadow and open back up the whole self.

* * *

Carl Jung said that the way to our authentic self was through the shadow. This is because the shadow contains all the material within ourselves that we have dissociated, denied and repressed. We disown it and push it into our subconscious, from where we then project it onto others. It is as if others are full of this disowned trait, while we glide through life completely free of it.

We are left with a false self; an inaccurate self-image; a self built upon lies that we have told ourselves about ourselves. This is why in order to reach our authentic self, we need to recognise and overcome the shadow.

We do this by contacting, recognising, re-owning and re-integrating the shadow elements into our full self, thus moving in the direction of authenticity. This healthy and functional self mustn't be confused with our 'real' self; our 'witness/I-am-ness' (see 'Become Witness' and 'Acceptance and Non-Judgement'), but it is the embodied vehicle through which the real self is expressed and communicates with the outside world. We thus need this embodied self to be as functional and as accurate and as authentic and as highly developed as it can be. If we were to express our true self through a false self, then the true self wouldn't find expression in the world; at least, it would be disfigured and dysfunctional.

What even those people who are familiar with shadow work don't recognise, however, is that shadow work can be either positive or negative. The previous chapter described the latter; this is often easier to spot. We're less used to dealing with the golden shadow, or the positive material, but in order to regain our true greatness, we must deal with the golden shadow in the same way.

Contemplate:

- Were you surprised to know that you could effectively give your greatness away to others?
- Have you been giving your self-confidence and highest qualities to a hero of yours?
- Do you feel a clearing-out in your psyche as a result of this work?
- Can you see that in order to carry out your mission in this life, you must use all the God-given qualities that you naturally possess?
- Note that the 3-2-1 process can be used for both the shadow and the golden shadow.

20

Know Your Genius

You are the salt of the earth, but if salt has lost its taste, how shall its saltiness be restored? It is no longer good for anything except to be thrown out and trampled under people's feet. You are the light of the world. A city set on a hill cannot be hidden. Nor do people light a lamp and put it under a basket, but on a stand, and it gives light to all in the house. In the same way, let your light shine before others, so that they may see your good works and give glory to your Father who is in heaven.
– Matthew 5:13–16

The Lord will fulfil his purpose for me; your steadfast love, O Lord, endures for ever. Do not forsake the work of your hands.
– Psalm 138:8

And we know that for those who love God all things work together for good, for those who are called according to his purpose.
– Romans 8:28

Listen to your being. It is continuously giving you hints; it is a still, small voice. It does not shout at you, that is true. And if you are a little silent you will start feeling your way. Be the person you are. Never try to be another, and you will become mature. Maturity is accepting the responsibility of being oneself, whatsoever the cost. Risking all to be oneself, that's what maturity is all about.
– Osho

Practice:

Think of 10 to 14 people who have known you for at least a couple of years. Preferably choose people who you've known since you were young.

You need to pick people who you do not work with, but preferably not close family. We need to find people who know you as *you*, i.e. not the job role you do. For example, you might be a great lawyer, but that might not be the real *you* – you might be doing something as a career that you felt obliged to do, rather than the thing that plays out your highest qualities – the gift that you were meant to give back to the world.

Send the people you have chosen an email, something like this:

> Hi [name],
>
> I am undertaking an exercise to discover my highest qualities. These are the things that you think that I'm good at; they might be personality qualities, or the way that I am with people or just those things about me that make me tick. I am looking to find the aspects of who I am that are my best qualities – things that I can seek to build upon and give back to the world.
>
> I am writing to you as somebody who has known me for a reasonable amount of time and who knows me well.
>
> Please just write down 12 qualities that you feel that I have. Keep it to just one word for each quality please.
>
> I really appreciate your time in doing this!

Once you have your results, put the words into a spreadsheet (or do this manually on paper if you prefer). To begin with, just put the name of the person who responded, and enter the list of words they gave you under their name.

Then copy and paste all of the words and put them into a single column.

Sort the column from A to Z.

This should begin to put similar words together.

Do a bit of manual sorting/sifting. If you have similar words, e.g. 'energy', 'driven', then group them if they have the same fundamental meaning.

Where you have any quality that is just a single one, that only one person has written, then discard that quality in the sorting process.

Now list the qualities starting with the one that most people have mentioned – typically this might be a word which 6–8 people chose about you. You will then get a few with 3–6 respondents typically; then a number with a couple of respondents.

This is the sorted list of your **top qualities**!

These are the **brilliances** that you have to offer the world.

Put together, they form your **genius**.

Now comes the contemplative aspect. Take time out, maybe over a few days, and keep your sorted list close by; print it out or copy it into notes on your smartphone.

Gently and gradually contemplate these qualities. What do they mean? Are you in the right day job to offer your genius to the world? Is the day job not the main focus of your life – are you living out your genius in other ways – volunteering, caring, leading groups, creative projects etc.?

Pray – ask Spirit to guide you.

Wait, seek, align.

God will shine light on this; the Angels will pave the way for you to live out your genius on this planet.

* * *

For some people, the word 'genius' seems a little overcooked for a list of positive qualities. But think about it – you haven't prompted the people you've asked in any way whatsoever.

There are over 60,000 adjectives in the English language – the fact that you can group some common ones that your friends have chosen to describe your qualities indicates that these really must be qualities that you have to offer the world. And given the immense number of words that could apply to any individual, the chances that any other person on the planet has the same list as you have is vanishingly small.

This is a really big deal! You are an eternal spiritual being living a very short life in human form in order to experience, to love, to show compassion, and to learn and to grow. God made you with this unique combination of qualities. This combination is therefore as individual to you as a fingerprint. So that has to mean something, right? This fingerprint therefore represents your genius in the world. If you find this difficult to accept, try looking again at the 'Golden Shadow' practice, and the words of scripture at the top of this practice.

Just consider this – how many times in a lifetime do you get a list of your own qualities in this way? Probably this is the first ever time (distinct from work-based 360-degree feedback exercises which mostly focus only on your ability at a particular job/task, and which are much more prone to 'projection' on the part of the observer).

So do not underestimate the importance of this. If you describe that combination of qualities as anything less than your genius, then you fail to understand the magnitude of this practice. Remember, though, that it's only really genius if you a) figure out what it all means when seen as a whole; and b) do something with it – put it into practice.

This is God talking to you. This is utterly exciting, exhilarating stuff. Honour this description of your personal genius. Grasp this and you've understood one of the fundamental lessons that your time on this planet has to show you.

Now for the small task of putting it out there into the world – see 'Live Your Mission'.

Contemplate:

- Did the list surprise you?
- How did it make you feel?
- Are you able to fully absorb this into your heart, or is there anything defensive in you that doesn't want to embrace it all? If anything is holding you back in accepting it, then just ask God to give you the gift of acceptance.
- Absorb the idea of honouring your gifts; they are given to you by the grace of God.
- Imagine what your life would look like in, say, five years, if you were to let the brakes off and fully let your genius flourish in your life to the maximum. Then pray – put your intention out there to let it be!

21

Live Your Mission

For it will be like a man going on a journey, who called his servants and entrusted to them his property. To one he gave five talents, to another two, to another one, to each according to his ability. Then he went away. He who had received the five talents went at once and traded with them, and he made five talents more. So also he who had the two talents made two talents more. But he who had received the one talent went and dug in the ground and hid his master's money. Now after a long time the master of those servants came and settled accounts with them. And he who had received the five talents came forward, bringing five talents more, saying, 'Master, you delivered to me five talents; here I have made five talents more.' His master said to him, 'Well done, good and faithful servant. You have been faithful over a little; I will set you over much. Enter into the joy of your master.' And he also who had the two talents came forward, saying, 'Master, you delivered to me two talents; here I have made two talents more.' His master said to him, 'Well done, good and faithful servant. You have been faithful over a little; I will set you over much. Enter into the joy of your master.' He also who had received the one talent came forward, saying, 'Master, I knew you to be a hard man, reaping where you did not sow, and gathering where you scattered no seed, so I was afraid, and I went and hid your talent in the ground. Here you have what is yours.' But his master answered him, 'You wicked and slothful servant! You knew that I reap where I have not sown and gather where I scattered no seed? Then you ought to have invested my money with the bankers, and at my coming I should have received what was my own with

interest. So take the talent from him and give it to him who has the ten talents. For to everyone who has will more be given, and he will have an abundance...
– Matthew 25:14–29

Everyone has been made for some particular work, and the desire for that work has been put in [your] heart. Let the beauty of what you love be what you do. Let yourself be silently drawn by the stronger pull of what you really love.
– Rumi

Practice:

Remember that God dwells in you.

Remember that you are as much a part of the Universe as any other part.

Carefully contemplate your gifts; your genius. Hold them up before God in prayer.

Remember that you are not praying for God to give you things, or to change God, but simply to affirm the truth that God dwells in you and wants to give you nothing but good. Prayer is a way of aligning your spirit of discernment with the heart of God.

So, align your gifts and your genius with your actions in this world. Turn your gifts into a practical mission. Do this with all the preparation and help of the Angelic realm.

Listen and feel for guidance within. Act with your heart.

Most of all: ACT!

* * *

Pablo Picasso once said, 'The meaning of life is to find your gift. The purpose of life is to give it away.' So, this is a two-stage process, to be used as a partner-practice with 'Know Your Genius'.

The reason that this is included in a book on Mind-Spirit Detox practice is that becoming close to Spirit is a practical endeavour; it involves doing something. Simply wallowing in the beauty of 'being' is never fulfilling enough, and for good reason. It's not the reason why we are put on this planet.

One of the most astonishing, spirit-filled people that I have ever encountered, the Reverend Walter Robbins, once told me that if you ever want to be truly filled in a supernatural way with the very essence of God, then you need to step out in faith into the world and give of yourself – then you will be filled until overflowing with God's grace and power.

Walter himself lived for 19 years in the remote Chaco region in northern Argentina, ministering to local Indians, the dispossessed, prisoners and so on. Many people came to know God through Walter's ministry with the South American Missionary Society. Walter used to recount how many people were healed by God of terrible maladies, such as cancer and tropical diseases. When you look into Walter's eyes, it is like looking into the face of Jesus himself, such is the radiance and love that emanates from him.

In a similar way, I was recently a guest on an American radio show, *World Spirituality*, on the Unity FM network. Half an hour before the show went on air, I suddenly had the most awe-inspiring spiritual encounter. I was transfixed as what seemed like a waterfall of cosmic power showered down on me for what seemed like ages; it was at once heavy with power, and also brilliantly and beautifully light and uplifting. The Holy Spirit came upon me, not because I asked for Him so that I could have a nice spiritual buzz, but because I needed the power and guidance of Spirit in order to step out of my comfort zone and give of my gifts.

This book contains many truths and many prayerful meditative practices. But it is not enough to know these truths – prayer and meditation needs to be accompanied by word and action. The importance of actually applying truth and love in our everyday lives and in gifting our genius to the world cannot be overstated. There is nothing more nauseating than somebody who talks about God and who attends a congregation, but who then doesn't demonstrate spiritual principle in their life.

Conversely, if we walk the talk daily, practise, learn, grow when we fall short, and live as Jesus showed us to live, then the true power of Spirit will bubble up inside us. Not only will our lives change beyond measure, but the Spirit of God will be poured out from us to reach the hearts of countless others. This is ultimately the true fulfilment of our lives here on earth. In study after study, it has been shown that the happiest people aren't those who earn the most or have the most possessions, but it is those people who know that they are fulfilling their life destiny.

When we align our genius and our consciousness with the perfection of God's consciousness, through prayer, contemplation and meditation, then we create the conditions for miracles to happen.

Therefore, when you have ascertained your gifts and your genius, go through the contemplation phase, then step out in the knowledge that the most incredible abundance of spirit will be turned on to illuminate your path.

Contemplate:

- Look back at your life. How much of it has already aligned with your gifts and genius?
- Do you need just a slight nudge on the rudder, or do you need to turn the ship around?
- If you've not fully aligned head, heart, soul, gifts and mission yet, then contemplate how life might look different if you had included God in your decisions in the past.
- How much different will life look in the future if you 'Align with the Divine'?

- Think BIG! As Woody Allen once said, 'The only thing standing between me and greatness...is ME.' Why copy this – why not reach for the stars?

22

Pour Out Your Heart with Blessings

God blesses those who are poor…for the Kingdom of Heaven is theirs.
– Matthew 5:3–10, NLT

Practice:
As you go about your daily business, just focus on your heart area.

With every in-breath, fan the flames of your heart.

Open your heart up; imagine that a window is opening and the love in your heart is flooding out.

And as the love flows out of the window of the heart, send it on its way with a blessing.

You may be in church, in a meeting, or walking down the high street.

Wherever you are, focus on individuals you pass, and send a wave of blessing towards them from the window of your heart.

* * *

This is a beautiful practice. It focuses on love and it brings your heart into alignment with the heart of the Divine.

God works through us. God has no feet or hands here on earth; the Divine uses ours! We are indeed blessed to be walking this beautiful planet at this time. Love is the unified field that binds all of creation. Enjoy the privilege of sending blessings of love to your fellow travellers.

Contemplate:
- How does it make you feel to do this?
- Do you feel the love you send out returning back to you?

- Does it increase your spiritual awareness?
- Do you feel the Divine flowing through you?
- Are you able to discern the hurts, the needs, the spiritual longing in those that you send waves of blessings towards?

23

Transformation

Do not be conformed to this world, but be transformed by the renewal of your mind, that by testing you may discern what is the will of God, what is good and acceptable and perfect.
– Romans 12:2

And we all, with unveiled face, beholding the glory of the Lord, are being transformed into the same image from one degree of glory to another. For this comes from the Lord who is the Spirit.
– 2 Corinthians 3:18

For as he thinketh in his heart, so is he.
– Proverbs 23:7, AV

Truth is not something outside to be discovered; it is something inside to be realised.
– Osho

Practice:
Set the alarm 15 minutes early tomorrow.

Remember to expect resistance. Therefore, the night before, write a note to put by the bed for yourself in the morning. Tell yourself to get up as you committed to doing something important: nothing less than the transformation of the mind!

When you rise, spend a minute or two in silence.

Sit upright. Take in the space in the room around you.

Now, ask God to come into your life on this day. Invite God to guide your thoughts; to cleanse your mind of unhelpful falsehoods and to help you focus on truth and beauty.

As you go about your day, be conscious of the movement of

thought hour by hour, minute by minute.

Affirm:

- Today I commit to the renewal of my mind.
- Today my mind turns only to what is good.
- Today I submit to the transformational power of Spirit.
- Today I fill my thoughts only with what serves my highest purpose.
- Today I consciously discern healthy thought and discard unhealthy thought.
- Today I forgive deeply.
- Today I feel peace, love and joy.
- Today I renew my heart with the power of Truth.
- Today Christ Consciousness expands to fill my every thought, word and deed.
- Today Spirit guides my thoughts which powerfully manifest as action in the world around me.

* * *

I challenge you to think of anything in the world around you that didn't originate in thought. Everything you see around you, all views espoused on the radio, all violence, all good deeds, all loving acts, all learning…everything that is created, everything that is manifest, started in thought. Thought transforms the mind; the mind transforms the heart.

We are co-creators with God; God created us, and He works through us. The reality that we create originates through our thoughts and beliefs. Because our minds are connected to the creative mind of God, we have the power to create our experiences by the activity of our thinking. This is expressed most coherently by Unity consciousness: 'Thoughts held in mind produce after their kind.'

We can see this all around us in the people we encounter.

Chapter 23

People who focus on jealousy, doubt, fear, lack and so on have lives that are filled with all of these things. People who focus on love, laughter, generative relationships, abundance, peace, creativity, meaning, gifts, forgiveness, expansiveness are filled with...guess what?!

We can therefore see that the type of energy, or vibrations, that we put out into the world through our thoughts, actions and intentions works rather like a magnet – the type of energy that we give out attracts similar energy in return.

Furthermore, what we focus on in our thoughts expands and multiplies. Therefore if we want a life filled with creativity, then we must consciously extend creativity to projects, people and the world around us. If we think small, it will remain small; if we aim for the stars, there's every chance that we might reach them.

Our brief sojourn as embodied humans on this beautiful planet is in large part for our benefit so that we can learn to grow closer to God. This is key to God granting us free will. We use this free will to turn away from negative thoughts, critical judgement of others, jealousy, victimhood and so on. We achieve true transformation when we align our thoughts instead with the Divinity of God; we then walk the path of abundance, expansiveness and infinite possibility.

Contemplate:

- Are you holding yourself back from your highest potential? Refer to the practice on 'Love and Fear' – reflect on whether it might be fear that is holding you back.
- Did you find it challenging the first day you tried this? If so, don't beat yourself up; this is a big deal and you might have to break a lifetime of unhelpful thought patterns. Try doing this in bite-sized chunks as it comes into your consciousness.
- Mastery of these techniques is elusive – treat this more like a journey, a process of moving towards an ideal rather

than seeking to arrive somewhere.

- Don't torture yourself if negative thought arises – observe it, acknowledge it, greet it like an old friend and then wave it goodbye.

- In time, continue the renewal of the mind by moving away from direct thought altogether. Open your mind simply to 'what is'. Try this: look at a flower. Truly look at it. Do not think of its name. Just see its beauty. But don't think of the word 'beauty'. Savour its fragrance, but don't think of the word 'smell'. Just experience it as if you've never seen a flower before. See it for what it is. How do you find this? Do you experience the flower in a more real, more vibrant way than before?

- In a similar way, instead of saying, 'I want a red car', or, 'I want to be more patient', just feel into the vibration of the reality that it might represent – move away from direct thought and direct language; dive into the reality behind what those symbols represent; move deeper to the metaphysical, fundamental layers of reality. When you connect with 'what is' on this quantum level, your prayers, your intentions connect more directly and more powerfully with the world of Spirit and possibility.

24

Deny Falsehoods

For although they knew God, they did not honour him as God or give thanks to him, but they became futile in their thinking, and their foolish hearts were darkened.
– Romans 1:21

Practice:

Write these statements down somewhere where they are easily accessible and say them repeatedly throughout the day and the week:

There is nothing in all the Universe for me to fear.

There is no Truth in evil; there is no evil in Truth.

I deny that life is hard.

There is no lack or limitation in my life.

Pain and sickness cannot master me.

This (condition, belief, situation) has no power over me.

* * *

Denials and affirmations are a meditative form of prayer that we can use to help align our heart-mind with God.

Affirmative prayer is a process of co-creation with Spirit that heightens and aligns our mind's connection with the mind of God. Through this alignment, Spirit brings forth abundant good, greater wholeness, and ever more clarity of our life purpose. We thus experience the blessings of greater spiritual expression in our daily lives.

One of the key things that we deny is suffering. We are eternal spirits living in human form, so we all will suffer from time to time. However, we can consciously decide whether or not to 'buy into suffering', i.e. to make it our life story, the background narrative of our life; or we can deny it. When we make suffering our story, we create useless, unnecessary suffering. Suffering is painful, but if we own the pain and suffer more because of how we have chosen to live with and identify with the pain, then this ownership and identification creates additional suffering which can be avoided.

This is why we deny the pain its power and its mastery. Pain does not own you. Avoiding pain in this life is sometimes impossible; but the second part of the pain – the ownership of it – is optional.

If you find it hard to deny the suffering, think of your life as if it were a movie. Then say to yourself, 'I don't want to be a part of this movie!'

Often, traditional forms of prayer come from the perspective of duality, i.e. small, insignificant humans trying desperately to get God's attention and then to plead with Him to give us favours. A more integral view of our relationship to God radically and beautifully alters this perspective. Therefore, prayer is not seen as a technique for changing and persuading God, but for expanding and transforming our minds, and thus changing the nature of our embodied spirit.

Affirmations and denials promote our development as integral beings by helping us to redirect our thoughts from mistaken beliefs in the power of appearances (such as thoughts of lack, limitation, separation, sickness), and to affirm the truth of our Divine connection to God and to all of life. Through brain-plasticity and repetition, affirmations and denials help restructure our subconscious mind and allow us to enter into a special state of surrender, receptivity and communion with Spirit, where we listen in silence for guidance and where we experience our connection with the Divine.

Contemplate:

- When you consciously reject self-limiting beliefs, contractions of belief and thought, can you feel the weight of unhelpful and unhealthy negativity rising from you?
- Can you see that this isn't your thought trying desperately to insulate yourself from reality, but it's actually about allowing distance from false thinking in order that Truth has space to flourish in your life?

25

Affirm the Truth

Therefore I tell you, do not worry about your life, what you will eat or drink; or about your body, what you will wear. Is not life more than food, and the body more than clothes? Look at the birds of the air; they do not sow or reap or store away in barns, and yet your heavenly Father feeds them. Are you not much more valuable than they? Can any one of you by worrying add a single hour to your life?

And why do you worry about clothes? See how the flowers of the field grow. They do not labour or spin. Yet I tell you that not even Solomon in all his splendour was dressed like one of these. If that is how God clothes the grass of the field, which is here today and tomorrow is thrown into the fire, will he not much more clothe you – you of little faith? So do not worry, saying, 'What shall we eat?' or 'What shall we drink?' or 'What shall we wear?' For the pagans run after all these things, and your heavenly Father knows that you need them. But seek first his kingdom and his righteousness, and all these things will be given to you as well.
– Matthew 6:25–33, NIV

What we think we become.
– Buddha

Practice:
Keep these affirmations close to you, where they are easily accessible. Look at the list, and choose maybe just three or four each week that either speak to you right now in your current circumstance, or are simply those that make your heart sing.

Say them repeatedly throughout the day and the week. Next week, maybe choose another one or two to replace some. Let your heart and intuition lead you.

- I expect good. I accept good.
- My heart is open to God's renewing love.
- The presence of God is within me and around me.
- I am free.
- God's healing love flows through me now, making me whole and free.
- I am centred in Spirit and nothing can disturb the equanimity in my heart.
- I am created in the image of God.
- I accept my healing right here in this very moment.
- I am God's beloved creation, and I rely on God's provision to fulfil my highest good.
- I am open and receptive to God's living Spirit.
- I am a child of God.
- I attract my good and radiate good to others.
- When I turn to Christ, I am filled with renewal and joy.
- My life is prospered and enriched through my relationship with Spirit.
- I am alive with creative energy, awake to prospering ideas and open to unlimited goodness.
- My knowledge of God makes me whole in spirit, soul and body.
- I am unlimited.
- I am God's creation, His perfect creation.
- I am a spiritual being, living in a spiritual Universe, governed by spiritual laws.
- I give thanks for God's guidance that leads me to live a life full of abundance.
- I am blessed with beauty and wholeness.
- I am part of the wholeness of creation, and I fully take my place, my rightful place, in the Universe.
- The creative flow of spirits floods my thoughts and the world around me.

- I am healthy and strong because I surrender to the healing power of Spirit.
- The peace of God settles upon me, upon my thoughts and in my heart.
- Divine love radiates from me to all around me.
- I am whole in God's presence. There is nothing here that should not be here; there is nothing missing that should be here.
- God's presence brings me to a place of perfect life and peace.
- The Kingdom of God is within me.
- I relax, release any anxious thought, and peacefully rest in the light of Spirit.
- I am whole and well in mind, body, and spirit. All is well.
- With my thoughts focused on love and abundance, I relish my journey of joyful living, and those around me see this reflected in my words and actions and in my face and in my eyes.
- God's will for me is perfect.

* * *

Denials (see 'Deny Falsehoods') create a vacuum in consciousness which needs to be filled with positive thoughts and feelings; therefore, it is good to follow up a denial with an affirmation.

It is important to note that affirmations in and of themselves are limited. They are a helpful tool that turns our thoughts away from self-limiting beliefs, and towards the truth, simply 'what is'. They are limited because, in one sense, they are merely words on a page. What they do, however, can be remarkable if approached in the correct way. By repeating them over and over, they take root in our minds and in our hearts. They crowd out limiting and unhelpful beliefs and help turn our minds towards the truth. In this way, while being limited in and of themselves, they point us towards expansiveness and a life lived in abundance.

We are conditioned from an early age by the media, by pessimists, and by the world around us, to think and retain negative thought within our heart and our soul. Some people purposely practise negative thought as a way of being – saying such things as, 'If I expect the worst all the time, at least I won't be disappointed.' But this type of thinking is dangerous and unhealthy. It's also contagious. Try to stay away from or at least limit your time with negative people. This book points towards the glory and beauty of this world and our place in it, when we are fully and properly orientated towards God and the truth that Christ came to teach us. If we hang around with negative, pessimistic people, we can so easily begin to adopt their insidious way of thinking.

So, surround yourself with spiritually and mentally healthy people as much as possible. Where you have to spend time with people who are filled with doubt and self-limiting thoughts, give them the gift of love of the knowledge of the Truth. Radiate this knowledge and truth to them. Trust that they will grow. If they refuse to budge, then try to stay away from them – they will not bring goodness into your life.

These affirmations, therefore, are a means of illuminating your mind with the truth of God. They are not attempting to transmit something that might be nice but which isn't a true reflection of this world. So, work with them; enjoy them, and let them fill your entire soul with the Truth of Being!

Contemplate:
- This is just the beginning – feel other truths arise, and write them down. Declare them out loud, say them, repeat them until they seep into your soul. Live from truth!

26

Life Review

There is nothing concealed that will not be disclosed, or hidden that will not be made known. What you have said in the dark will be heard in the daylight, and what you have whispered in the ear in the inner rooms will be proclaimed from the roofs.

– Luke 12:2–3, NIV

If anyone hears my words but does not keep them, I do not judge that person. For I did not come to judge the world, but to save the world.

– John 12:47, NIV

Practice:

Lie still. Close your eyes.

Focus on your breathing.

Let your thoughts settle.

If thoughts arise, just let them pass, like clouds drifting in the sky.

Continue to still your mind. Relax your body.

Think back to early childhood; think of your first memories.

Feel into yourself as you were; feel into your relationships with close family members and friends.

Feel into situations you experienced: waking up in the morning; your dreams; playing with toys; playing games outside.

Now think about your time in school. How did it feel to be you? Think about your hopes and your aspirations; think about your school work; remember the smells and the friends and the sounds.

Remember the triumphs and the defeats. Remember the good

in you and the not so good.

Now continue to cast your mind over your life: your early adult life; your relationships; your family, the people that you influenced; the people you hurt; the people you brought great joy to.

Continue to focus on your breathing as you do this.

Now bring yourself right up until the present day. Think about the last ten or so years until this present moment.

How are you right now? Are you bringing light into the lives of those around you? How far does your circle of influence extend?

Now go back over the whole story of your life all over again. This time, though, come away from the 'me', the 'I', and look at yourself through the eyes of those people whose lives you touched when you first thought about your own life. Move from the first person to the third, from the 'I' to the 'he/she'.

Continue to look back at yourself through the eyes of others – your parents or carers; your siblings if you had them; your friends; your teachers; your colleagues.

What do you see?

Do you see love?

Do you see forgiveness?

Do you see wisdom?

Do you see purpose?

Do you see patience?

Do you see warmth?

Do you see connection?

Do you see kindness?

Do you see generosity of spirit?

Do you see God?

Now, just relax a moment.

Again, turn your focus to your breathing.

Now continue to extend from this moment and into the future. What do you see in your future self?

Look through your own eyes.

Now look through the eyes of others.

What do you see?

How will you affect others in the future?

How are you going to have maximum impact in your time on earth?

Think about the major lines of human development. Are you maxing out on each of them? In your personal development, consider how you are doing. Where do your gifts lie? Is there a line of development that you could concentrate on expanding and stretching?

Here are the major lines:

- Cognitive
- Intrapersonal
- Emotional/interpersonal
- Somatic/kinaesthetic (relating to the body)
- Moral
- Spiritual
- Willpower

* * *

Note in particular the latter line of development – willpower. This one transcends and connects all others. The mere fact that you are reading this book and engaging with the practices indicates that you must have some degree of willpower and a sense of development. Know that you can increase your willpower; it becomes like a habit, it can be built in as a natural part of your day-to-day existence. When you become familiar with the flow state, and begin to align your mission and purpose, you will be able to enter into a natural rhythm of spiritual and personal development. You will engage with productive practice that is aligned with your higher good, and it will no longer feel like work, even if you expend much energy and many hours on your chosen activity.

The life review is something that is common to nearly all deep Near-Death Experiences. You are led to see your own life in its entirety through the eyes of others. You feel deeply the joy, the hurt, the pain, the sorrow and the laughter that you cause others.

None of this is done in a judgemental manner. It is done to inform and educate you. It is part of your learning. One of the reasons that we are here on earth is to experience and to learn. This is a learning experience...you simply cannot learn and grow as pure spirit – that's why God placed us here and why not everything is perfect on earth. If it were perfect, if we had no struggles, then we couldn't learn. And besides, spirits cannot taste chocolate...there are some distinct advantages to being here!

When we begin to awaken from the fog of the drama, the banal drudge of what can be daily life, and begin to helicopter above all of it and recognise why we are put here; to recognise our gifts, our purpose and our mission, then we begin to see the point of it all.

So why not conduct this beautiful little self-audit; a check-in with your own spirit, from time to time. In that way, we're recognising why God placed us here in the first place; why this world is perfectly designed to be a wonderful classroom for the soul. So, honour the Divine creator in doing this exercise. Do it with a spirit of exploration, of wonder, and also with a spirit of creativity. Even if you know that there are things you could have done differently in the past, remember that your thoughts can mould the future, so try to project the learning from the past into your contemplation of the future.

Remember – do not judge or condemn yourself. Just see, just feel. See it for what it is. It is what it is. Just let it be.

Contemplate:

- How does it feel to see yourself through the eyes of others?
- Was there a disparity between the way you saw yourself and the way in which other people saw you?
- Were you able to see yourself without judging? To accept that you cannot be perfect; that your imperfections are indeed the very material of learning for you?

27

Align with the Divine...and Shine!

For God, who said, 'Light shall shine out of darkness,' is the
One who has shone in our hearts...
– 2 Corinthians 4:6, NASB

What you seek is seeking you.
– Rumi

Practice:

Take a deep breath.
Still the body.
Still all thought.
Concentrate on the breath.
With every breath, relax deeper.
As thought arises, bless it and send it on its way.
Return to the breath.
Focus on the window of the heart.
See and feel the light within your heart, the light that is love.

Know that the source of love, the Kingdom of God, is within you.
The heart centre is the very Kingdom of God.
You are an intrinsic part of that Kingdom.
Without you, that Kingdom would not be complete.

Now align your heart centre with the heart of God, the heart of
the Divine.
Build up that love.
Build up that light and let it shine.
Feel the light in your heart getting stronger, getting brighter.
The light is love, pure love.

Let the beauty of your love shine.

Feel the love shining within your heart.

Radiate love back out into the world of form as a beautiful beam of light, through the window of the heart.

On the in-breath, build up the light.

On the out-breath, shine that light out into the world.

You are pure energy, pure light, pure spirit.

Let this knowledge grow from your heart and radiate back out to the world as light.

Love the light that flows from within you, and radiate the light on a wave of blessing.

And as you connect with the light of the heart centre, experience the Unity of all, the connection between the world of form and the world of Spirit, of formlessness.

Let the light of the Universe cleanse and renew your heart.

Align with the Divine in this very moment.

Know that the Divine is pure energy, pure light, pure love, and shine that light out into the world.

Connect with the one true God, and reflect that glory with every breath.

Let it be so!

* * *

Many of us will have been brought up in fear-based religions. These give us a sense of dread, of unworthiness, of doubt about our place in eternity.

When we truly Align with the Divine, we welcome the very spirit of God into our soul. And here's the secret – it was there all along, we just didn't recognise it! The spirit that is within us has no fear; it is just blinding light, it is brilliant love, as Paul says here in Romans 8:15 (NASB):

Chapter 27

For you have not received a spirit of slavery leading to fear again, but you have received a spirit of adoption as sons by which we cry out, 'Abba! Father!'

So, free yourself from any bondage, any slavery, any fear, and truly know this practice; say it to yourself in your heart every morning and every evening for a week. Make a note of the effect it has on you. Live from this place every day. It will change you and it will change those around you.

Contemplate:

- Are there moments you can think of where if you had 'Aligned with the Divine' and shone your light, things might have turned out better for you and/or the people around you?
- Be aware of those moments as they arise in the future. If you ever find yourself in a situation where you are being driven by negative thoughts or feelings, and feel any contractions, just think, 'Align and Shine!', and do this practice wherever you are.

28

Grow Tall!

The righteous will flourish like a palm tree, they will grow like a cedar of Lebanon...
– Psalm 92:12, NIV

You were born with wings. Why prefer to crawl through life?
– Rumi

Practice:

Reflect on the following:

This moment right now is perfect.
You have everything you need.
This is the very point from which you need to grow.

Do not try and change reality;
See what is here, and let it be.
Simply allow what is moving through you to move.

Does a tree ask itself every year,
'Shall I grow a little taller this year, or would that be selfish of me?'

So just rest in this beautiful reality,
Rest as the beautiful person that God created,

And allow yourself to shoot for the stars,
Be the creative and loving force that you always wanted to be,
Because those thoughts, those instincts, were placed there by the Divine.

Chapter 28

Honour them,
Grow Tall!

* * *

Comfort can be a curse. It can lead to complacency and lack of ambition and growth. It can lead to us being self-deprecating and feeling as if we are not worthy of great things. So keep on moving; allow the energy that is moving through all things to take flight in you right now and from now to eternity. In this way, we honour the Divine creative energy that is in us.

Contemplate:
- Imagine what your life would look like if you let all of the energy of spirit flow through you with no hindrance.
- What would you do?
- How would life feel?
- Imagine love flowing through you – how would this affect those around you?
- How tall could you grow?

29

I Acknowledge the
Feelings in My Heart

Keep your heart with all vigilance, for from it flow the springs
of life.
– Proverbs 4:23

Come, seek, for search is the foundation of fortune: every
success depends upon focusing the heart.
– Rumi

Practice:

Keep a daily diary for a week.

Write in it any strong feelings you have during the day.

Write down the feelings in your heart.

Write down a very short narrative of why you felt that way.

After a week, have a look at what you have written.

* * *

Emotional blockages to 'self' can be a major impediment to
moving forwards with God. If you try to let the Divine in to your
heart, but are cut off from your heart yourself, can you see how
the latter might inhibit the flow of Spirit?

People are often staggered at how varied their emotions are
across the course of a day. Some cultures, such as the British,
or many organisational cultures, teach that it is good to steady
one's feelings, to be neither too happy, nor too angry, nor too
sad. Because there exist corporate and community cultures that
pressure us not to show much outward display of emotion, we can
therefore often respond by actually suppressing these emotions,

not merely to just hold off from revealing our emotions to others.

When we deny our true feelings to ourselves as well as to others, we cut ourselves off from an important aspect of reality. If we stop consciously recognising our own emotions, how much more difficult will it be to recognise the moving of subtle energies such as the prompting and guidance of Spirit? Get in touch with yourself, and you also facilitate the opening of the heart to God.

Therefore, the intention of this practice is to reveal to yourself the real 'you', and in so doing, to open the window of the heart to the movement of Spirit.

Other positive aspects of keeping a feelings diary include the fact that it:

- resolves trauma
- helps us make sense of the world around us
- releases thoughts and feelings
- helps us lighten our spirit
- reduces stress
- helps to develop one of our key lines of intelligence, i.e. Emotional Intelligence
- helps us to recognise other people's points of view
- helps to bring healing.

Contemplate:

- Were you surprised by what you discovered about yourself?
- Do you recognise that you were somewhat cut off from your heart?
- Do you feel more of a sense of forgiveness with yourself for the range of emotions that you discovered?
- How do you feel that being in touch with your heart might help facilitate a closer walk with God?

30

You Are the Universe; You Are Home

All things were made through him, and without him was not any thing made that was made.
– John 1:3

You are not a drop in the ocean. You are the entire ocean in a drop.
– Rumi

Practice:

Go and sit on a bench where you have a clear and expansive view of the horizon. This can be inland, or preferably overlooking the sea.

Be still.

Stare intently as far as you can see.

Now widen your view to take in the whole of the horizon.

Widen your view further to take in all of your peripheral vision at once.

Remain like this for a while.

See it all.

Be it all.

Now widen your vision again to take in what you cannot see. In your mind's eye, see beyond the horizon; know the places beyond. Continue to expand your view further, further. Take in the sky. Take in what is beyond the sky, the heavens above, and the earth in its entirety.

Rest.

Now know, truly know, that you are one with all that is.

This is your home.

Chapter 30

You belong here.

Nothing and nobody and no belief can take that away from you.

It is your birthright.

You are home.

This is yours, as much as it is anything or anybody else's.

You are made from the stuff of the Universe.

You are the Universe.

You are as much the Universe as anything else you can see or discern.

There is no separation.

Everything you see is imbued with the breath of God.

There is nothing here that isn't part of the Universe.

And that includes YOU.

* * *

This practice came to me from Spirit one time when I was sitting on a bench overlooking the botanical gardens by the sea in Lyme Regis in Dorset. It was an incredible revelation to me. I'd always held the thought that I somehow was separate from God. That I didn't belong. That I was an outsider trying to seek reconciliation and connection with the world around me and with God.

While meditating, I suddenly discovered that I was truly home, that I was truly a part of the Universe myself; it shattered so many self-limiting beliefs that I'd picked up down the years. This earth, this Universe, is my home! This is mine, I belong here!

In this moment of revelation, I had experienced what is known as 'non-dualism', which points to the idea that the Universe and all its multiplicity are ultimately expressions or appearances of one essential reality.

This has its roots in Eastern philosophy, but when applied to Christian tradition, it brings an expansive, positive and inclusive viewpoint to scripture and begins to bring beauty and harmony to our knowledge of Truth.

It's also worth noting the scientific reality behind this practice. It is an inescapable truth that we are truly one with the Universe. We are literally made of stardust!

All of the material that we humans are made of comes out of dying stars, or stars that died in massive explosions, which are supernova. Supernova explosions occur frequently somewhere in the Universe and from time to time can even be seen from earth such is their brilliance and magnitude. (Source: Schrijver and Schrijver, *Living with the Stars: How the Human Body Is Connected to the Life Cycles of the Earth, the Planets, and the Stars.*)

So there you are, this exercise just connects our awareness with what actually is scientific fact. It also connects us with the truth of who we are in the Universe, the Universe that is made by, and is one with, God. Note also that this practice links with the truths in the practice, 'Unity'.

Contemplate:

- As you live your life for the next week or so, be conscious that everywhere you go is truly home for you. You totally and utterly belong here.
- How does that make you feel? Has anything profound shifted for you?

31

Know Only the Truth

...and you will know the truth, and the truth will set you free.
– John 8:32

Enlightenment is a destructive process. It has nothing to do with becoming better or being happier. Enlightenment is the crumbling away of untruth. It's seeing through the façade of pretence. It's the complete eradication of everything we imagined to be true.
– Adyashanti

Practice:
The truth and reality of God and Spirit is binary in its nature. God or Spirit is either true or it is untrue. So many of us cling to this truth by faith alone.

We sometimes need the faith because doubt can be so strong in our minds.

We sometimes need doctrine because we don't trust our own hearts.

However, not all doctrine sits comfortably inside us; instinct sometimes tells us that either it's only a partial version of the truth, or it's a distortion of the truth, or at least that the underlying truth behind the words of doctrine might have been altered somewhat by its application.

The essence of doctrine in any event has been strained through the filter of history, of politics, and of language, and as with any metaphysical notion, it can be robbed of its deeper, underlying meaning. Certainly, it is easy to struggle under the complexity of doctrine. We shudder at the words of fear, of doubt, or of our own essential unworthiness.

If any of this rings true for you, then this might just be one of the most essential practices in this book.

Clear your head of all teaching, all dogma, all doctrine.

Begin with meditation and let it segue into contemplation.

Sit silently; sit still.

Settle the mind by concentrating on your breathing.

With every out-breath, go deeper into relaxation.

With every in-breath, take in the love and the knowledge of 'What Is'.

'What Is' must be The Truth.

There is no teaching,
There are no other people,
There are no rules,
There is no fear,
There is no mind,
There are no words,
There is no history,
There are no thoughts,
There are no memories,
There is no tradition,
There is no past,
There is no future.
There is only NOW.
This 'now' is eternal.
Nothing else exists.

Be in this 'now'.
Be the 'now'.

If any thoughts crowd in upon you, just let them go.

Now just gently meditate upon the truth of simply 'What Is'.

Open the window of your heart and let the love and truth of

Chapter 31

Spirit fill you right now, here in this perfect moment.

There's no need to *believe* when you *know*!

Did you have to believe in your mother or your father?

When you were a child, did you have to believe in their love?

No, you knew them; you felt their presence.

In the same way, just let the pure knowingness fill every corner of your being.

Revel in the knowledge and in the love of 'what is'.

This 'what is' is the very nature of God.

It is the beating heart of the Universe.

Its nature is Divine Love.

This is no tiny parcel of information; what you are experiencing is the essential creative life force of the Universe itself.

It IS the Universe.

It IS Divine Spirit.

It IS God.

It Just IS!

Just BE.

Just KNOW.

Spend as much time as you can, knowing, loving and 'being'.

It's beautiful, isn't it?

When you're ready, slowly open your eyes, have a little stretch, and go about the rest of your day. Over the next week, you might like to revisit this meditation, but most importantly, let the reality of the knowledge of God that you now have sink deeper and deeper through contemplation.

* * *

As you go about your daily business and let the experience of this practice seep into your heart, let the lessons grow inside you. Let the true, pure knowledge of God marinate every atom of your being. Feel how it is to truly stop and know God. Not *think* about God; not understand what others say you must know or think about God; not strive to overcome doubts about God. None of these things can hold a light to the glory of actually *knowing* God. And when you *know* God, you no longer need to hold on to faith or belief. For what use is faith or belief when you have *knowledge*?

Remember the binary nature of God, as stated above? Faith and belief contain seeds of doubt; the possibility that there is no God. When you attain true knowledge of God, there is no doubt left. Doubt within knowledge is an oxymoron. It can't possibly be present if God is simply 'What Is'.

You have now discovered that God, or Divine Spirit, isn't a concept; it isn't just a thing that might be nice to have in your life. It isn't about any institution or tradition. It is simply the true, fundamental, absolute essence of *What Is*! God simply *IS*! So in your contemplation, recognise that everything you see or feel or perceive; all love; all grace, all gratitude, all of life – the people, the animals, the earth and the heavens; all that is seen and unseen – all of this is God. God and God's nature is all around you – in you, outside you, in everything. In fact, there isn't anything you can experience that lies outside the domain of *What Is*! God is so big that you can sometimes miss Him/Her! It's like an ant walking on the hull of a superliner. The ant doesn't see the ship as it's just so expansive. It stretches out into all directions.

So go, live your life, give your gift, and with an open heart know at all times that Divine Spirit is all around. Know it, truly *know it*! There is no longer any place in your heart for doubt. Throw it away, as it no longer serves your higher good.

Contemplate:

- How does this knowledge change your view of God? How does it change your view of yourself?

32

Receive Guidance

But when He, the Spirit of truth, comes, He will guide you into all the truth; for He will not speak on His own initiative, but whatever He hears, He will speak; and He will disclose to you what is to come.
– John 16:13, NASB

There is a voice that doesn't use words. Listen.
– Rumi

Practice:
When you're struggling to know God's will, or even at times when things are good for you, and you could do with some extra guidance, find yourself a quiet place and sit or lie.

Focus on your breathing and let your eyes shut.

Let clean, renewing air fill your nostrils and lungs on the in-breath. With the out-breath, feel any used-up, old energy leaving your body through the soles of your feet.

With the in-breath, take in fresh, clear air; with the out-breath, push old, used-up energy out of the soles of your feet.

Just continue this for a while.

Deepen your breathing with every in-breath.

Feel the body relax as it is renewed. Feel the old energy leave the body and feel refreshed by the flood of new, clean, bright energy.

Now, gently, say in your mind, say to yourself, 'Higher wisdom now'; repeat it three times.

Rest.

Now say to yourself, 'Awareness now'; repeat it three times.

Rest.

Imagine the wings of an Angel enfolding you.

Look within.

Feel.

Expand your awareness; know that wisdom is within you.

Feel into that awareness.

Feel into that wisdom.

Allow yourself to fully know the truth; to know the path.

Come away from your head and feel with your heart.

Rest.

Listen.

Let the Christ Spirit within you guide your heart.

* * *

Our essence is of God; we are created fully by God. There isn't a cell in our body that lacks God's essence. Therefore, we are inherently good. This 'God essence', called 'The Christ', was fully expressed in Jesus.

All of us have the spark of God within us – this is the Christ Spirit within.

As we are created in the image and likeness of God, we are always connected directly to the indwelling Presence of Christ without needing anyone to intercede for us. Jesus said that the Kingdom of God is within us, so we need to turn within to find the Christ Spirit and our higher wisdom. Spirit's guidance and wisdom is attainable by stopping, clearing out the old interference patterns and the unhelpful energy, and just letting our awareness expand. When we do so, we move away from concentrated thought, and into the heart centre, where true wisdom resides.

Therefore, when we turn inwards, we receive guidance directly, and we are always worthy to receive God's good. We have the potential to follow the example of Jesus who shows us how to perfectly express our Divine nature just as he did, and thus become a clear conduit for the flow of God's Love in the world.

Contemplate:

- It can be useful to have spiritual mentors and guides, but have you ever confused this with unhelpful thoughts about human hierarchy? What might you need to do to return to a healthy view of equality before God? When you do this, do you see that God's guidance lies within you?

- Some people say that the most difficult journey in the world is from the head down to the heart. How do you find it?

33

Connection

Behold, I stand at the door and knock. If anyone hears my voice and opens the door, I will come in to him and eat with him, and he with me.

– Revelation 3:20

Practice:

Be still.

Keep your eyes open.

Be aware of what is here in this place.

Maintain your gaze.

Let your focus begin to rest not upon objects but upon space… the space in the room around you. Focus on the nothingness that is the space.

What is here? What is to be found in the space? Anything? Nothing?

Be aware of the silence of the space.

Rest into the silence.

Now wait.

Be aware of the see-er; the 'I-am-ness' at the core of your being.

See with this awareness.

Keep on waiting.

Do not wait with any expectation. If any thoughts float into your awareness, just bless them and send them on their way.

Just continue to wait.

Do not expect anything to happen. Just BE.

Continue to rest.

Be pure awareness.

Be pure resting.

Be pure waiting.

* * *

Chapter 33

This meditation is a beautiful way to connect with God. The focusing on space takes our mind away from the movement of thought and helps us focus on nothingness. Focusing on nothingness is rather paradoxical; funny, even. How can you focus on a thing that is not a thing?

Well, if I tell you not to think about pink elephants for a minute, the chances are you'll be tortured by trying not to, but they'll keep on popping up into your head. I just asked my daughter to do this and she said that they arose in her thoughts about ten times within the minute!

So if I ask you to think about absolutely nothing for ten minutes, you might have a similar experience. However, by focusing on space, you can think about 'nothing' without the torturous aspect of being forced to stop thought. So you do indeed effectively stop thought, but you do so the easy way!

This isn't an end in itself; it merely begins to condition the mind. The important point is about to start – just resting in silence and waiting. Waiting without any expectation. Meditation is not a means to an end – it can't be because there is no end, no arrival.

This is the mistake made by people trying to find enlightenment. Again, they torment themselves with this – with this constant thinking about something that doesn't really exist; how do you know when you've got there? What would it look like; what would it feel like? Nobody really knows; there is certainly no common definition. You may be so addicted to the process that you wouldn't want to stop even if you stumbled upon this thing known as enlightenment.

That is why I prefer to speak of 'awakening'. Awakening is a process, not a destination. Awakening is the revelation and realisation of the reality of who you are and your relationship with God. It is something that can only ever happen in the 'now', in the present, when we are present to this very moment.

Connection with God happens when we just stop long enough to notice; when we stop the continual movement of thought, and move into the space that is outside of time, there we find love; there we find connection with the Divine.

Contemplate:

- Can you see the importance of waiting without any expectation? God will come to you in line with His perfect timing and will. If we meditate with thought and expectation, then we are putting yet another human barrier up between us and Him. Create space and you create the seeming nothingness within which Spirit dances.

34

Listen Like the Mountains

Know this, my beloved brothers: let every person be quick to hear, slow to speak, slow to anger...
– James 1:19

This exercise is in two parts. Whenever your partner or your children or somebody close to you has something to say, LISTEN!

Practice:
Part 1

When somebody is talking to you, don't add anything from your side. Just listen.

Listen with all that you have.

Sure, say, 'OK', 'yes', 'hmm' and so on, just to reassure them that you're present, and haven't drifted off!

Maintain eye contact; but add nothing else – don't say anything; don't fix anything; don't comment, and above all, do not judge.

Just stay wide open with a vast, still but powerful consciousness, as big, vast, and as strong as the mountains; but remain silent as the mountains are silent.

Be completely with the other person. Just sit and wait, but when they speak, REALLY pay attention with every cell in your body.

This brings out trust in the other person. It brings stability and love to the relationship.

This silent stage should last just 3–5 minutes.

Part 2

Now comes the more active listening part.

You don't add any interpretations or judgement, but you do speak, in a way that elicits more information from the other person.

Exercise the practice of curiosity.

Be genuinely curious. Don't try and get depth. That would only give you an agenda. If you're simply curious, then you get a natural deepening.

Ask curious questions to elicit more depth.

At no point do you need to add any comment or judgement. Just be there for the other person. They will know that you have listened and understood. Sometimes that is all that is needed.

* * *

Note: Before you do this exercise, you can prepare yourself by going outside and practising 'pure listening'. You are listening without any purpose as such; listen to the sounds outside for just 5–10 minutes – catch any sound in the environment – birds, traffic, rustles of wind. You can do this while keeping your eyes open and your attention outward – this is not a meditation. Just try to catch every sound by extending your awareness far outward; try to hear sounds as far away as you can. This will attenuate your hearing, and prepare you well for this exercise.

Deep listening is something that we so rarely do, especially to our loved ones. This exercise is a powerful way of connecting profoundly with those we hold most dear, and indeed for anybody that we wish to have a meaningful encounter with.

We are all addicts to non-listening. We're addicted to our own voices, to distraction, to multi-tasking etc. The reality is that you simply cannot do anything at the same time as properly listening. When you really listen, you do so with *all* of you. There is no space for anything else.

There's something deeply sacred and transformative to be

able to tell the truth when somebody else is deeply listening without judging. If somebody really pays you attention, you feel really obliged to be truthful. This is one of the surprising aspects of being the deep listener; just how deeply you can travel into pure heart truth with your partner or friend.

Many of the exercises in this book are around knowing ourselves and knowing God. We do this through fully entering into the truth of who we are and the truth of the nature of God. In this way, we begin to heal the relationship. This practice is similar. Through absolute listening, it heals and brings life to our relationships with other people. We create a space of stillness, peace, connection and understanding. Spirit enters into such places. Spirit will be with both of you when you connect in this way.

Enjoy this, and practise; it will become a habit eventually, but you may have to overcome decades of poor conditioning. Practise as often as you can for a few weeks whenever the opportunity arises.

Contemplate:

- When you practise this, how does it make you feel?
- Do you have to overcome any internal resistances to practise this?
- Do you notice any changes in those that you deeply listen to?
- If doing this practice with a family member or your partner, do you feel a deeper sense of love?

35

I Bring My Whole Self to This Moment

Now as they went on their way, Jesus entered a village. And a woman named Martha welcomed him into her house. And she had a sister called Mary, who sat at the Lord's feet and listened to his teaching. But Martha was distracted with much serving. And she went up to him and said, 'Lord, do you not care that my sister has left me to serve alone? Tell her then to help me.' But the Lord answered her, 'Martha, Martha, you are anxious and troubled about many things, but one thing is necessary. Mary has chosen the good portion, which will not be taken away from her.'
– Luke 10:38–42

Do not be conformed to this world, but be transformed by the renewal of your mind, that by testing you may discern what is the will of God, what is good and acceptable and perfect.
– Romans 12:2

Practice:

Stop!
Stop whatever you are doing at least once a day.
Stop for about five minutes if you can.
Drop whatever you're doing.
Be still.
Listen. Listen intently until you hear with all of you. Try to discern even the faintest sound. Close your eyes. Imagine that you're in a bowl with 360-degree speakers; pick out whereabouts in this sphere the sounds are coming from. Pinpoint the sound.
Be nothing but hearing.
Keep your eyes closed. Just feel. Feel with all of you. Feel

your body wherever you are; feel the clothes; feel whatever is touching your body; feel the breath in and out of your nostrils; feel the weight of your body on the chair or the bed or the ground.

Be nothing but feeling.

Open your eyes now. Remain very still. Look forward. Look as far as you can, whether it be the horizon or the other side of the room. Keep looking straight, but widen your awareness now to include everything to either side, above and below. Widen your awareness to include everything in your field of view. Maintain your gaze. Look within, look around and look beyond. Shift your awareness until you truly see.

Be nothing but seeing.

Gently close your eyes again. Turn inward now. Who is hearing these things; who is feeling these things? If you find, 'me', or 'self', or 'I', then turn away from them and ask yourself the question, 'Who is aware of the "me" or "self" or "I"?'

Keep on going deeper and deeper until you cannot see the see-er. Keep on going until you find nothing but spaciousness and pure awareness, pure serenity.

Be nothing but awareness.

* * *

I saw a cartoon today which prompted this meditation. The cartoon was entitled, 'Why dogs are happier than us'. The setting was a hillside with trees. The owner had a thought bubble filled with all manner of deeds, expectations, worries, thoughts, dramas and calculations. The dog? Well, it had a thought bubble that exactly mirrored the scene – the hillside with trees. Simple. Nothing added, nothing taken away.

Thought can be a wonderful thing – it was thought that created books; buildings; computers; the judicial system; industry, finance, transport and so on. But thought can also crowd out our very experience of *being*. We live lost in the past, or anticipating the future; we miss the only thing that is essentially real – this moment! You will never and can never ever live in the past or in the future – it's impossible. You only ever live in the eternal present. The eternal present is the only reality that it is possible to exist within.

This practice therefore connects us at least daily with the reality of the moment. Fortunately, this can be done with little effort. Practise it every day for 20 days and it should become a habit. You don't have to take yourself away from the world to do it. Simply at some point in your day, find just a few minutes to see, feel and hear. It will reconnect you with your senses, with your embodied being. Then as you turn inwards and seek the inner self, you will reconnect with your true self; pure 'subjective' being; the pure 'I-am-ness' inside, pure spirit.

This is your fullest self – and it is totally connected with the present moment; the truest reality of existence. You are now anchored in yourself, your true self; fully connected in space and time.

It is in this space of connectedness with yourself that you most fully meet with God. If you are disconnected from this moment and disconnected with yourself, and your relationship with the outside world is broken by the incessant churn of thought, then how can you expect to connect with Spirit? This is a healing practice. It heals broken bonds between us and the world outside and the truest self within us – between our senses and our awareness. It heals and brings wholeness; this is the beginning of true freedom, the freedom of *being*.

Contemplate:

- How much of your life is disconnected from reality, from yourself, from Spirit?
- Recognise how damaging thought processes can be when they are not used consciously, how much of your waking moments are lost in abstract thought.

36

Joy in the Moment

I perceived that there is nothing better for them than to be joyful and to do good as long as they live; also that everyone should eat and drink and take pleasure in all his toil – this is God's gift to man.

– Ecclesiastes 3:12–13

That is the simple secret of happiness. Whatever you are doing, don't let the past move your mind; don't let the future disturb you. Because the past is no more and the future is not yet. To live in the memories, to live in the imagination, is to live in the non-existential. And when you are living in the non-existential, you are missing that which is existential. Naturally you will be miserable, because you will miss your whole life.

– Osho

Practice:
Whenever you do something very difficult, challenging, scary, or even something wonderful and expansive, always start by saying these words to yourself:

'I choose to feel joy in this moment.'

* * *

Imbuing a moment or a challenge with this affirmation can be incredibly powerful. I have used this personally on many occasions over the past few years. On no occasion has the outcome been anything other than uplifting and surprising.

Firstly, by affirming the words, 'I choose', you are positively stating that you are making a personal commitment to make a choice. You are also affirming that it is your right to make a choice. The opposite might be that you choose nothing; that you leave your heart response open to the winds of fate. By asserting the personal right to make a choice, you might not be able to affect everything in the external world, but you are certainly preparing to take conscious control of how you respond internally. It's not what happens in the world around us that makes the difference; it's how we respond where the magic happens.

Furthermore, by using the word 'joy', you are affirming that it doesn't matter what the exterior world holds in that moment for you – you are inducing a heightened sense of positivity, compassion, love and vibration. You commit the moment to the highest good of Spirit.

Lastly, you are focusing on the moment. Not any other moment, but this moment. You choose to let *this* moment in and of itself be a unique point in time.

I love this practice – it's simple and powerful, and it never wears out – use it again and again!

Contemplate:

- When you have faced difficult moments that have induced trepidation in the past, has your negative, worried approach helped or hindered you?
- If you've practised this exercise when you've been confronting a difficult situation, how do you feel it changed the outcome?

37

Die to Self

If then you have been raised with Christ, seek the things that are above, where Christ is, seated at the right hand of God. Set your minds on things that are above, not on things that are on earth. For you have died, and your life is hidden with Christ in God. When Christ who is your life appears, then you also will appear with him in glory. Put to death therefore what is earthly in you: sexual immorality, impurity, passion, evil desire, and covetousness, which is idolatry.
– Colossians 3:1–5

Therefore, if anyone is in Christ, he is a new creation. The old has passed away; behold, the new has come.
– 2 Corinthians 5:17

Die to everything of yesterday so that your mind is always fresh, always young, innocent, full of vigour and passion.
– Krishnamurti

Time to cash in your chips, put your ideas and beliefs on the table. See who has the bigger hand – you, or the Mystery that pervades you. Time to scrape the mind's shit off your shoes, undo the laces that hold your prison together and dangle your toes into emptiness. Once you've put everything on the table, once all of your currency is gone, and your pockets are full of air, all you've got left to gamble with is yourself. Go ahead, climb up onto the velvet top of the highest stakes table. Place yourself as the bet. Look God in the eyes and finally or once in your life, lose.
– Adyashanti

Practice:

Standing up, look out at nature – your garden, the park, the sea, the horizon; by day or by night. Look upon your life. See the rhythm and the pulse of the life that you have lived. See the glories and the heartaches. See the pain and the joy. Scan your own history.

Know that you have built up a lifetime of judgements, of jealousies, of words that should have remained unsaid, of people you have hurt, of things not done that you should have done; of people you should have comforted but chose not to.

Now let it all go.

Kill the old self.

Surrender to the feeling of letting it all go in the most complete way possible.

Just kill the old soul. Leave your body alone of course! Kill the inner soul; like a snake shedding its skin. Let it go.

Let it go.

Rest in the nothingness of death for some time.

When sufficient time has elapsed, gradually return to the earth again.

Rebirth the new!

Wake up again to a whole new world, a whole new YOU!

Walk back into the world as if rebirthed into heaven.

Heaven here on earth.

Let your glory shine.

Be at one with the heavens above.

* * *

This is an extremely powerful experience, and not something to be done on a whim when you have little time. Meditate on it and keep it in your heart until your intuition tells you it is time. I really must emphasise that any death/killing is merely metaphorical! Having said that, if this exercise is approached from the perspective of as real a death as possible, then its effects are profound.

The Bible is peppered with references to surrender and sacrifice; however, it is difficult to appreciate just how powerful the reality of this practice is until you actually experience them. In carrying out this practice, you will experience for yourself, maybe for the first time, just what these words that you may have read a thousand times actually mean. It is a visceral experience like no other.

Contemplate:

- I'd encourage you not to do this exercise as soon as you read it. If you feel compelled to do it immediately, then that's great. However, it may be best to give it a little time. Contemplate it for at least a few days prior to doing it. Build it up; give it the seriousness and sanctity that it deserves. Make a ceremony of it. In that way, you will get much more from it; its full power will be released.

38

Heaven Is Here!

And Jesus replied, 'I assure you, today you will be with me in paradise.'
– Luke 23:43, NLT

Never lose an opportunity of seeing anything beautiful, for beauty is God's handwriting.
– Ralph Waldo Emerson

Practice:
Go to a special place in nature. Climb a hill, walk a coastal path, seek solitude in the forest.

Imagine that you have passed from this life, and that this is your first day in heaven. God has given you a familiar place to be, to begin with, as you take your first steps in paradise.

Feel the beauty of the place that is heaven. Marvel at the sanctity of this place. Crouch down and study the flowers, the leaves.

Feel the plants speaking to you.

Feel into your body and revel in its connection to the world around you.

You are in heaven.

All is well.

Stay in this place for as long as you can. When you meet other people, or return to an area of habitation, greet others as eternal souls, sharing the bliss of heaven.

* * *

This is one of my all-time favourite practices. It follows on well from the 'Die to Self' practice. It came to me years ago, taking a lunchtime stroll along the cliff path west of Budleigh Salterton in East Devon. I wasn't seeking the experience, it just happened, as if I truly had just passed to the other side. The dappled light of the sun broke through the canopy of leaves above me, the air was heavy with the scent of pine; I was quite alone, and God came to my heart. He said, 'Don't just wait for heaven. Know that I am with you now; enjoy this sacred planet that I have created for you. Heaven is already here – just open your eyes and your heart and truly see it. It's always been here, but you are too busy to recognise it.' What a truly blissful moment.

This isn't a practice that I do very often; maybe only once or twice a year. However, it is so, so powerful that it stays with you. It truly changes you.

Contemplate:
- How much of heaven is already here, all around you? In the beauty and complexity of creation; in love and laughter and in friendship?
- Have you been missing this?
- How does it feel to connect with it again? How does it feel to have this revelation sink into your consciousness?

39

Practising Nothingness

For those who live according to the flesh set their minds on the things of the flesh, but those who live according to the Spirit set their minds on the things of the Spirit.
– Romans 8:5

You can get rid of all this insanity created by the past in you. Just by being a simple witness of your thought processes. It is simply sitting silently, witnessing the thoughts passing before you. Just witnessing, not interfering, not even judging, because the moment you judge you have lost the pure witness. The moment you say, 'this is good, this is bad', you have already jumped onto the thought process...as you become more and more deeply rooted in witnessing, thoughts start disappearing. You are, but the mind is utterly empty. That's the moment of enlightenment. That is the moment that you become for the first time an unconditioned, sane, really free human being.
– Osho

Practice:
When you're in the supermarket or in the mall, be invisible.

Imagine when you enter the store that your presence, your 'being', expands and expands until it fills the entire store.

And as this expands, the visible 'you' contracts.

It disappears to the point where you are no longer seen in your physical body.

So your spirit expands and your physical body disappears.

Thus you become the everything and the nothing.

As you wander around the store, just be conscious that you are the observer. You are not the observed.

Notice how little anybody looks in your direction.

You could be invisible.

But your spirit is enormous, casting blessings on everything around.

* * *

This is a fascinating and fun exercise. The remarkable aspect of it is that you can enter into such a different realm of consciousness while doing something as mundane as shopping. You can be in the same familiar space that you know so well, but your self-image can be enormously shifted.

So many of us are trapped in a Point of View, a habitual pattern of self-limiting behaviour, that says, 'They are all looking at me.' The reality, as you'll discover in doing this practice, is that nearly all of the time, absolutely nobody is looking at you. The unique aspect of this practice is that in imagining that we are invisible, absolutely nothing changes. Merely the perception that you might have had previously that everybody is looking at you disappears, as we recognise that this Point of View never held any truth.

The absolute reality is that you yourself rarely really focus intently on anybody when you're out and about. People somehow tend to fade into the background. The same is true of you when you're living your life. Nobody particularly notices, unless you're going out of your way to make some kind of an impact. Sometimes even then, people either don't notice or they pretend not to notice. One New Year's Eve we were going to a fancy dress party called 'Arabian Nights'. My friend, Rafael, was dressed in a rather elaborate Persian Prince outfit. He wanted to stop off at the corner shop to buy some cigarettes on our way, so he swept into the shop as if he were straight off the set of *Lawrence of Arabia*. When he emerged I asked him if the shopkeeper had remarked on his outfit. 'No, he didn't even blink an eyelid,' Rafael said, much to my astonishment.

This practice, then, is also helpful in enabling you to concentrate upon just living your life and being free within your own skin. It might not resonate with everybody, but there are such a huge number of people who are weighed down by the false notion of self-consciousness. This self-consciousness is often worn as if it were a cloak, and this cloak can serve to insulate us from our truest nature, and our truest nature from Spirit, hence the importance of the practice.

If this resonates with you, let this practice be in your constant toolkit of practices until it is habituated and no longer serves a purpose as a discreet exercise.

Contemplate

- How often do you get the feeling that everybody is thinking about you, or looking at you, or judging you?
- If these feelings arise, recognise how this exercise helps you to break away from these limited beliefs and to sink into your own true nature.

40

Transcendence

For you created my inmost being...
– Psalm 139:13, NIV

We realise, often quite suddenly, that our sense of self, which has been formed and constructed out of our ideas, beliefs and images, is not really who we are. It doesn't define us, it has no centre.
– Adyashanti

Practice:

Sit quietly.

Still the mind.

Focus on your breathing.

Let all tension leave your body with every out-breath.

Let all thought float away like a puff of smoke on the breeze.

Now, focus on an object in front of you. Do so in the usual way, with your awareness coming from within your head, from the focus of your eyes and the interpretation of the brain. Continue to look from within.

You are observing; you are the observer; you are the witness, and the witnessing is stemming from within your head, within your physical being. Your witness is from the inside towards the outside.

Now, keep your focus on the object but, this time, just imagine that you have no head. Your awareness is simply floating on top of your shoulders. Your awareness is located outside of your physical being, somewhere in the region on top of your shoulders.

Continue to focus intently on the object from this space

outside of yourself.

Maintain your focus.

Experience the sensation of becoming one with the object. There is nothing to divide you and the object; you are on the same side as the object now. You are one with what you observe. There is nothing between you and the object.

There is no longer the observer and the observed. There is only 'what is'. Look around you. Become one with any object you see.

Getting wider and wider, widen your awareness. Expand your awareness to include all of the room. See all of the room at once; widen your awareness to take in every corner of the room.

You are no longer *in* the room.

The room is inside *you*.

Rest as that.

* * *

So, this shift of awareness from within yourself to outside of yourself results in the culmination of a kind of rebirth into a new experience where the false identity of separation begins to dissolve.

You may experience some kind of an epiphany, or you may have to repeat the practice several times to let the new awareness emerge, but whenever you get the breakthrough in consciousness, you are becoming one with the absolute Awareness of Being right here and now.

The written interpretation of this is problematic, because words stem from a sense of mind that operates in thoughts and images. As Truth or Spirit is directly known outside of the realm of words, trying to describe it would be like a lie trying to explain truth using a lie! So try to avoid thought-based interpretations; just rest in the experience alone. I often muse about how we will experience Spirit when we have passed to the other side. It makes me laugh to think that people might be sitting around trying to formulate new doctrine to explain what they are experiencing. Of course we won't be doing that! We will be just revelling in the love and the ecstasy of being; we will absolutely *know* the truth without recourse to lengthy epistemologically brilliant theological treatises.

Now, think about God for a minute. Spend a short while thinking about God. What do you see? The most basic of answers, the juvenile answer, might be some kind of old man with a beard sitting on a cloud. A more sophisticated answer might be 'Spirit'. But neither of these quite gets to the absolute truth.

If a false identity of 'self' is perpetuated, then there will continue to be an observer – 'you', and the observed – 'God'. There is still the notion of two things; 'you' and 'God'. Where there is an 'and', there are two things, two objects.

This experience of 'witnessing' God is like an illusion trying to peek at Truth, but it is not Truth itself. That is why it is often so short-lived when we try to do it – an indication that this experience is not Truth, for if it were, it could not change – and the false sense of 'me' ends up in another illusion where 'it' then is trying to interpret and describe what 'it' thinks truth is according to what 'it' saw or witnessed. This cannot be the Truth; it has to be a kind of an illusion, like our seeing objects from within our physical body and thinking that we can really experience them.

Now, the question arises: If my experience is the product of a false sense of 'me', a false identity, then what do I have to do to transcend that false sense?

In a book of practices, the answer, paradoxically, is 'nothing'. I have consciously kept this practice back until the end of the book, as it reveals a higher principle at the heart of all the practices.

In and of themselves, practices are not the Truth. They simply serve to begin to re-program our sense of who we are in ourselves

– our true, absolute or higher nature; they shift awareness of who we are in relation to those around us; they increase the flow of love and abundance, and re-program our knowledge of the Divine. The practices lead us to absorb principles of Truth, thus promulgating higher consciousness. But even that is illusory, and therein lies the paradox, which I will come on to.

The reason why this is the final practice is that we have passed from the transactional, i.e. dealing with our own inner thoughts and feelings, and dealing with the world around us; to the transformational, i.e. letting Spirit transform who we are at the deepest level; our relationship with other people and with God.

This practice takes it one step further, towards the Transcendent.

Let me explain. Lower levels of practice develop from the belief that there is a person, a 'me', that is initially ignorant but can be brought to awaken to Truth. Yet, true awareness or 'I-am-ness', or pure 'subjectivity', does not conceive of 'separate identity apart from what I Am'. There is no such thing as 'higher or lower consciousness'. There is only One Consciousness. Thus, anything an illusory sense of 'me' is trying to do or achieve is still illusion.

So why is there nothing I can do in terms of practice to achieve transcendence? The reality is that 'I' does not exist in Truth. Universal consciousness is already fully aware and complete. Truth is 'I am'. The false sense of the egocentric 'I' cannot have a spiritual realisation, for this small 'I' doesn't exist in Truth. It therefore in truth is unable to become aware. Awareness itself is the only thing that really exists – this being interpreted, for example, as eternal presence, one-consciousness, peace or stillness.

As Shakespeare said, the human experience seems like a play on a stage. The people on the stage – the sense of separate little identities – seem like the actors. We can use this analogy as a practice to step into this nothingness of awareness. In this case, we can practise breaking free from the stage and moving into the audience as Step One. In so doing, we are moving from being the actor into being the observer. Stage Two that follows is to move beyond even this point. Let us move into this practice.

* * *

Step One, then, is to rid ourselves of the full sense of identity as an actor on the stage. Think back over your day in the office or at home. Think of the room that you were in and the people that you were with. Imagine that both you and all of your colleagues are the actors in a play.

Now imagine that you were looking upon this as a dispassionate observer. Imagine that you were a playwright and that what you observed of yourself today could be altered. Imagine that you could change the script of the play through thought.

Yet, using thought via the medium of prayer or meditation or imagination to change the script of the play that was your life today only creates another play, another room that starred you as the actor today. The same sense of 'I' is still present in the play. So we remain trapped within the same sense of thought that is false.

Therefore it is thought that is at the root of the problem as it creates the sense of a separate 'I', a separation that is not rooted in Truth. So, if thought is the problem, how do we escape the false sense of 'I' using thought? Put another way, if thought is the problem, how can it be the solution? How can we enact this practice without engaging simply in another practice of illusion? How do you escape the paradox? At first this might seem impossible. However, there are ways of escaping from this illusion.

Thus we continue the practice: Turn around, away from the room that you were in today, and look for the exit door. In so doing, you are turning away from the actors themselves as well as any narrative or action.

You may find that yet another room appears, and so we find that we cannot exit the room without leaving false identity behind. Before despair sets in, recognise that it is false identity that wants to exit, and the way is too narrow to fit through. It is illusion trying to exit illusion; a lie trying to exit a lie. Of course this cannot be done.

Instead of the seemingly eternal struggle to come into realisation of Truth, to leave the false sense of 'me' behind, now reject any 'doing', any 'effort'. Think of this as a kind of a non-practice. This is the practice of doing no-thing.

Relax. Leave activity behind you. Leave thought behind you. As we have already described, thought is the problem, not the solution.

Now take this even further. Reject that you are 'rejecting' or trying to discover anything. Reject the notion of 'doing'.

Move away from the illusion that there is a 'me' or an 'I' that is able to do any of these things.

Recognise that there never was such a 'me'. There never was a theatre, there never were stages or actors or observers. There was never a room that you were trying to escape from.

Be still. Recognise that if you still have the sense of a 'me' who can think of stages and actors and rooms and then is trying to deny all of this, then that is not Truth yet!

Truth does not know of anything that it is not, for It can only be what It is. One could say that the true experience of life is to be 'What Is' and there can be no concepts or knowing of what *isn't*.

* * *

There is no separate identity from I Am. Thus you have *transcended* the level of separation; the knowledge of who you are is no longer an object that you can observe; nothing of self can any longer be observed; separation has been *transcended* into the realm of pure subjectivity, i.e. the subject is no longer separate from the object.

However, as stated in earlier practices, we are called in this life to a) know our purpose and b) to give it away in our mission. We simply have to go about our daily life being 'embodied'. If we are to enter into this messy business of life, then we cannot avoid being a player on a stage. But we should view these stages with a shrug of our shoulders and let go of our struggle and involvement as much as possible and be still to that sense of 'me' with all of its feelings of lack, of plenty, of achievements and of failure.

Sink into this knowledge. Knowing who you really are is psychoactive in nature. This is not in the pharmacological sense. It means that simply knowing this begins to activate our mind and our brain-plasticity to enable the knowledge to take us to the next level of understanding and being.

So, the paradox is to practise this most profound of practices which is essentially a 'non-practice': it takes practice to get to the point of realisation that full knowledge of Truth requires no practice!

Contemplate:

- How did this move you?
- Did you find that the illusion of separation melted away?
- How does it feel to realise that there is no barrier in awareness between you and other people?
- How does it feel to shift your awareness away from your physical body?
- Are you able to exit the stage while still remaining embodied and living your mission in the manifest realm, i.e. the real world?

Bibliography

Dr Eben Alexander, *Proof of Heaven: A Neurosurgeon's Journey into the Afterlife*

Arjuna Ardagh, *Better Than Sex: The Ecstatic Art of Awakening Coaching*

Arjuna Ardagh, *The Translucent Revolution: How People Just Like You are Waking Up and Changing the World*

Bob Berman and Robert Lanza, *Biocentrism: How Life and Consciousness Are the Keys to Understanding the True Nature of the Universe*

William Buhlman, *The Secret of the Soul*

Eric Butterworth, *Spiritual Economics*

Eric Butterworth, *Unity: A Quest for Truth*

Jeremy Campbell, *Grammatical Man: Information, Entropy, Language and Life*

Matthew Fox and Rupert Sheldrake, *The Physics of Angels: Exploring the Realm Where Science and Spirit Meet*

Joel S Goldsmith, *The Infinite Way*

Annie Kagan, *The Afterlife of Billy Fingers: How My Bad-Boy Brother Proved to Me There's Life after Death*

J. Krishnamurti, *The First and Last Freedom*

Ervin Laszlo, *Science and the Akashic Field: An Integral Theory of Everything*

Bruce H Lipton, *The Biology of Belief: Unleashing the Power of Consciousness, Matter and Miracles*

James Marion, *Putting on the Mind of Christ: The Inner Work of Christian Spirituality*

Brian D McLaren, *A New Kind of Christianity*

Steven Pinker, *The Better Angels of Our Nature: The Decline of Violence in History and Its Causes*

Richard Rudd, *The Gene Keys: Unlocking the Higher Purpose Hidden in Your DNA*

Ronald Russell, *The Journey of Robert Monroe: From Out of Body Explorer to Consciousness Pioneer*

Karel Schrijver and Iris Schrijver, *Living with the Stars: How the Human Body Is Connected to the Life Cycles of the Earth, the Planets, and the Stars*

John Selby, *Expand This Moment*

Rupert Sheldrake, *Morphic Resonance: The Nature of Formative Causation*

Thomas M Sterner, *The Practicing Mind*

Ken Wilber, *Integral Spirituality: A Startling New Role for Religion in the Modern and Postmodern World*

Ken Wilber, *A Theory of Everything*

About the Author

Richard C Anderson MA, BSc (Joint Hons), DMS

For more information about Richard C Anderson, and his work as a Certified Awakening Coach, please search for Awakening Coaching UK on Facebook, or visit www.awakeningcoaching.co.uk

You will also find meditations inspired by Mind-Spirit Detox, as well as an opportunity to practise one-to-one or group Reiki meditation on Skype. Check out the linked YouTube channel for scores of spiritual book reviews and bonus Mind-Spirit Detox practices.

For corrections, book orders, author appearances, enquiries or interviews, contact the author at info@awakeningcoaching.co.uk

Awakening Coaching UK

Take Me To Truth
Undoing the Ego
Nouk Sanchez, Tomas Vieira
The best-selling step-by-step book on shedding the Ego, using the teachings of *A Course In Miracles*.
Paperback: 978-1-84694-050-7 ebook: 978-1-84694-654-7

The 7 Myths about Love...Actually!
The journey from your HEAD to the HEART of your SOUL
Mike George
Smashes all the myths about LOVE.
Paperback: 978-1-84694-288-4 ebook: 978-1-84694-682-0

The Holy Spirit's Interpretation of the New Testament
A course in Understanding and Acceptance
Regina Dawn Akers
Following on from the strength of *A Course In Miracles*, NTI teaches us how to experience the love and oneness of God.
Paperback: 978-1-84694-085-9 ebook: 978-1-78099-083-5

The Message of A Course In Miracles
A translation of the text in plain language
Elizabeth A. Cronkhite
A translation of *A Course in Miracles* into plain, everyday language for anyone seeking inner peace. The companion volume, *Practicing A Course In Miracles*, offers practical lessons and mentoring.
Paperback: 978-1-84694-319-5 ebook: 978-1-84694-642-4

Thinker's Guide to God

Peter Vardy

An introduction to key issues in the philosophy of religion.

Paperback: 978-1-90381-622-6

Your Simple Path

Find happiness in every step

Ian Tucker

A guide to helping us reconnect with what is really important in
our lives.

Paperback: 978-1-78279-349-6 ebook: 978-1-78279-348-9

Dying to Be Free

From Enforced Secrecy to Near Death to True Transformation

Hannah Robinson

After an unexpected accident and near-death experience, Hannah
Robinson found herself radically transforming her life, while a
remarkable new insight altered her relationship with her father, a
practising Catholic priest.

Paperback: 978-1-78535-254-6 ebook: 978-1-78535-255-3

Readers of ebooks can buy or view any of these bestsellers by
clicking on the live link in the title. Most titles are published
in paperback and as an ebook. Paperbacks are available in
traditional bookshops. Both print and ebook formats are
available online.

Find more titles and sign up to our readers' newsletter at
http://www.johnhuntpublishing.com/mind-body-spirit

Follow us on Facebook at https://www.facebook.com/OBooks/
and Twitter at https://twitter.com/obooks